i

CREDITS

Mississippi State University Instructional Media Center
Nancy Bardwell, Dorothy Johnson, Darion Evans
Louise and Paul Hughett
Shirley Shaw, Editor

For:
Benjamin Sarver, Garrett Sarver, Ryan Sarver, and Kenley Reaves

Cover photo: Javan Reaves

My Wonderful One, Baby boy, Javan "Grindflu" Reaves, Always on
the grind. Making it happen. Javan, for the day that you looked into my
eyes and said, *"You got to come out the box, Momma!"* I did. This book
is out-of-the-box for me, son. I had to cry and relive some very unfortunate events but this work is for all the disadvantaged, misled, illegitimate and abandoned children who are crying, "Oh, Father, where are
you?"

O' FATHER WHERE ART THOU?

DAUGHTER'S DESPERATE CRY

SON'S DEEPEST DESIRE

The Fatherless Antidote

GRACE SWIFT

DIMENSIONSNPUBLISHING

CONTENTS

FATHER'S POEM

Father, Father, reveal Yourself to me.
I have no prior knowledge of what father is
suppose to be. The first one left before I knew him,
so, that left my chances slim.
Mother married once, when I was a small girl.
but he, too, soon left this devastated my world.
There was one more chance for me to know
but he was a man who would often come and go.
In and out of my life but I'd never sat on his knee,
so how much of a father could he possibly be?
Yes, I had food and I had clothes
but, Father, Father that's as far as it goes.
Never any love, advice or closeness I could feel.
So, I'm still seeking a father, for one I know is real.
Will You speak to me, talk to me and show me what I missed?
'cause out of the three, not once have I been kissed
Can't remember a hug or the muscles in his arm,
Or one who would hide me in the midst of a storm.
When the battle got heated, or I faced a test,
I had to stand, alone hoping for the best.
Days have been long, I've had my children too,
So all I'm asking Father, "Please let me learn from You."
Before my eyes grow dim and I cannot see,
God, please, show me Father, and what father is supposed to be

Father's Day …2008

O' FATHER WHERE ARE YOU

This was my desperate cry. Pain was embedded so deeply within my heart that my mouth could not find words adequate enough to utter. I called upon Him twice. I say twice because I am too ashamed to be honest with even myself and admit that it was an uncountable, unbelievable number of times. Washing over me the entire course of my life it was parallel to the force of the wind of a hurricane. And yes, it has left brutal emptiness: That hopeless feeling that harasses me every year at this same time. It was Father's Day, again. Over fifty of them had come and gone and still, there was no one that I could call Father.

The ache within the soul cries out loud over and over again, "Father, Father," because that place, that space within is still too deep and yet the hunger that constantly nagged and cried so loud until it drowned out every good thing within, stifled every good thing intended towards you, and slaps a death blow to every opportunity that even pointed itself in your direction. So now after compounding all these years that overwhelming, all consuming "father lack" continues to increase. Decades have come and gone and the gap in that void lingers, in fact it widens. Trickling down it is devouring the youth and still gaining momentum because His presence is the only antidote to fill it, make the necessary corrections to satisfy the deep longing, the aching that has grown so out of control.

This wound from "father lack" is so vast until it has devoured generations and has erupted in every culture. His absence has secured a position so very far away from the element of family units all over this earth that there is no measuring device to reach him. There is no medication or medical instrument to remedy, nor political legislation to correct, no economical dollar amount to satisfy his debt. Neither is there any social program implemented to repair what has been produced in one act of pleasure in the bedroom.

Health and healing, wealth and solutions to all the above mentioned agencies and organizations are summed up in one word; Fatherhood. No, make that two: Father's presence.

Although phones are smart enough to reach thoughout the entire universe, navigate anyone to any location, it cannot find him. It holds the answer to every question, obtainable in mere seconds, but it cannot give a reasonable excuse, nor answer the question of his whereabouts. This universal reaching device in a child's hand matches the pain in his heart when his father's distance is beyond reach. No amount of technology on any phone can heal or help the bleeding wounds of these multiple millions of fatherless children. All of the elements within all the electronic devices put together cannot make up for the touch of his hand, the smile on his face, the embrace of his arms, or a word from his voice; Father.

One day the heart of the fathers will return to the children and the heart of the children to their fathers.

MY FATHER

He had remained in Tennessee when our house burned to the ground as we migrated to Indianapolis, Indiana. Mother had reminded my brother, Richard, in no loving words, how much he looked like his ugly daddy every time he did something that displeased her. But no matter how ugly momma said he was I longed for him. I wanted to see his face for myself. So many days I'd rehearsed what I would say when I saw him. So although I had not seen my father, WC Brown, since I was a toddler, it was no wonder that early one morning I was able to pick him out on a street in Franklin, Tennessee, where I was born.

My aunt, without my mother's knowledge, brought me to Tennessee when I was about eleven to attend my great grandmother, Susan Swift's funeral. To this day I have no recollection of anything that was said or done at grandma's funeral. I fought my way through the pain and suffering with the family but the only thing sorrowful for me were the seemingly unending hours that it took to finally bury her. Relishing in my private thoughts of how he'd treat me and love me, his baby girl put a smile on my face that no amount of grief and suffering could diminish.

Each mile that we drove back towards him, I felt the agony of the years that I had lived without him, his smiles, his touch, his protection, direction and loving care melting away as ice colliding with a burning torch. After the funeral service, burial, repast, family pleasantries and well wishes were over, we finally arrived at his house.

11

Running thru the door, I began to call out, "Daddy, daddy!" No answer. "Daddy where are you?" As I turned to face his faint "grunt" of an answer, no one could ever phantom the devastation I collided with and the torment inflicted upon me. He was drunk, so drunk that he was not capable of lifting his head, or opening his eyes to even look at me. The only thing that shielded me from my incessant pain was the deep sleep I had silently cried my way into.

So we resumed our six-hour journey back to Indianapolis where I'd spend the rest of my years in fatherlessness. Throughout my adolescent years, each time I'd recall his actions, or lack thereof towards me, that same gripping pain would terrorize me, forcing me to act out in diverse ill-mannered, negative behaviors.

It's a small wonder that the United States statistics on fatherlessness are as crucial as they are; mounting use of drugs, alcohol and substance abuse, illicit sex, and unruly behavior that places restraints on education, wellbeing and healthy lifestyles. It is the main cause of unlimited time in correctional and other institutions, causes suicide and senseless loss of many young lives. I had more than my fair share of the pain and lived that same hopeless helpless existence for too many years.

According to the statistics below (that anyone can easily obtain, Google: Fatherlessness) fatherlessness is a growing problem that continues to escalate. One thing about statistics is that they only deal with numbers and believe it or not there are always some that have not been counted. The devastation in the hearts and lives of these "Left behind" children can never be captured or demonstrated with figures.

There is always someone with you who will never leave you nor forsake you

US FATHERLESS STATISTICS

1.43% of US children live without their father [US Dept of Census]

2.90% of homeless and runaway children are from fatherless homes.
[US D.H.H.S., Bureau of the Census]

3.80% of rapists motivated with displaced anger come from
fatherless homes. [Criminal Justice & Behavior, Vol 14, pp.
403-26, 1978]

4.71% of pregnant teenagers lack a father. [U.S. Department of
Health and Human Services press release,

5.63% of youth suicides are from fatherless homes. [US D.H.H.S.,
Bureau of the Census]

6.85% of children who exhibit behavioral disorders come from
fatherless homes. [Center for Disease Control]

7.90% of adolescent repeat arsonists live with only their mother.
[Wray Herbert, "Dousing the Kindlers," Psychology Today, January,
1985, p. 28]

8.71% of high school dropouts come from fatherless homes.
[National Principals Association Report H.S.

9.75% of adolescent patients in chemical abuse centers come from fatherless homes. [Rainbows God's Children]

10.70% of juveniles in state operated institutions have no father. [US Department of Justice, Special Report, Sept. 1988]

11.85% of youths in prisons grew up in a fatherless home. [Fulton County Georgia jail populations, Texas Department of Corrections, 1992]

12. Fatherless boys and girls are: twice as likely to drop out of high school; twice as likely to end up in jail; four times more likely to need help for emotional or behavioral problems. [US D.H.H.S. news release, March 26, 1999]

If you love children as much as I do, you've probably viewed these stats with some degree of pain tugging at your heart. From which scenario is your view? Are you the mother who is left to daily look into the face of your abandoned child? Are you the mother forced to pay the taxes from your hard earnings (depriving your own children) in order to cover for that absentee father? Are you the missing father who is causing this duress for a child and his or her mother, government and society? What about the man who is picking up the slack for that deadbeat dad, is that you? My heart and prayers go out to you, if you are that child "left behind" crying, father, father as I had for so many years?

Growing up a fatherless child I know the inward struggle. It's too intense to contain within so it seeps out into many different areas, spills on many different people all over society, crippling too many families. It's like the pressure mounted in an aerosol can when punctured, the contents sprays out everywhere or even that carbonated soda being shaken up that erupts into undetermined, uncontrollable amounts and places.

Either way, I viewed this from several different positions myself. I have felt the pain from every female's perspective in the fatherlessness model: the mother, the wife, divorcee, the child and the worker.

At this point I will also add that I have held positions as a Correctional Officer in a prison hospital, psychiatric ward mainly, and a Youth facility, a Probation Officer, Victim Services Coordinator (Domestic Violence), Case Manager (facilitating group discussions in a Substance Abuse residential housing facility). I have volunteered my services for the Justice Coalition, serving innocent victims of violent crimes, and a volunteer for almost 25 years as a prayer minister for a telephone prayer line, in a position to intercede in prayer for people in the most heartbreaking, devastating situations.

In all of these heart-rending situations, facing all of the pain and suffering I've had to face over three decades has given me insights into the lives and brokenness of helpless and hopeless lives. Too many times, in each of the positions I've been placed either professionally or as a volunteer, it is all the same: in too many cases the people involved are a product of, or their situation was created as a result of, fatherlessness. All too many brutal, unexplained acts of destruction, violence, disruptive behavior and ill treatment can be traced back to this lack.

All over the world you will have tribulation; but be happy, there is always a light that shines in the darkness

FATHERLESSNESS HISTORY

Let's go to the place where, believe it or not, Jews and Muslims have common ground or at least they both can relate: Abram and his lovely wife Sarai. Abram desperately wanting a son, an heir to his vast fortune, but he has a barren wife unable to produce a child, at all. God actually promises him that he will have a son. To remedy their situation Mrs. Abram comes up with a "bright idea" that is the perfect solution to all their problems. She would assist God Almighty with His plan through another woman, get another woman pregnant and I will take ownership of that child. So Abram submits to wifey and sure enough a child comes into fulfillment.

Sarai pressured Abram into bearing a child with another woman, a slave. While Abram was awaiting a Promise from God, his wife controlled their situation and orchestrated something, someone apart from the promise or the Word that God had given to His chosen future father. Because of her desire a child was brought into Abram's life prior to God changing him into father "material": Abraham. Seems he had had that moment of pleasure that ushered him into a position of producing life but still, he had not yet been made into a father. Too many children are prematurely born into the lives of Abrams and Sarais.

DESIRES OF THE HEART AND FLESH

From fourteen to sixteen years of age the human body operates at its peak performance. Every member and organ in the body is in the most excellent condition for its highest performance level even for parenthood: sperm meeting egg. A natural God-given, God-ordained order (if you will). During those teen years everything vital to producing a child is the strongest.

The physically powerful magnetic force that draws them together comes through the physical senses such as touching and feeling, certain foods, watching certain things of sexual content, in pictures, hearing them in music, or through meditating on them through the mind and thought processes. Ever wondered how an eight-year-old boy feels aroused by looking at pictures of naked women. Why does her nakedness affect that particular member of his body? Even he cannot explain the reason. How does just watching sex awaken certain feelings in the human body? A touch from someone you love puts you in a mood that affects the reproductive organs.

All too often a young girl says, "Oh, I don't need birth control, I'm not having sex" and the next month (could be as early as the next day) she is pregnant. This happens all too often: A young girl awakens in the morning not having any thought of having sex and by night a sperm is fertilizing her egg. Needless to say how it got in her.

GIRLS GIRLS GIRLS

Here are some scenarios I've heard about girls from boys and brothers. The **good or pretty** girl is playing the role, living in denial like their parents. Flirting and stooping to anything to get her way, she goes beyond her limit to be number one. Not telling mom and dad that she has a change of clothes in the backpack, lighter in the pockets, love letters in the books, and loose cigarettes in her socks. Mom and dad have never taught her how to live without. She has always had everything her way and does not know how to handle life unless everything is to her advantage. So, any guy gives her a "pretty" little lie, just what she requires.

The **bad or ugly** girl is out aggressively seeking your good little boy. Dressing provocatively, thinking it makes her look better, trying to compete with the beauties, not making any apologies or excuses for what she plans to do. Bold and low enough to settle for just being told that she's beautiful. She will stoop to anything to stay in the game. Allows a boy to do anything he wants to do. She set herself up as easy prey, so the boys knows to tell her a "big beautiful" story.

The **So-called Christian** girl will play clean and innocent while she waits in the shadows for her turn. She is sly, cunning and patient enough to wait while she observes everyone who makes a mistake and she knows how to capitalize on it. When the other girls fail a guy or leave a broken or wounded heart she consoles and uses her "compassion" to manipulate what she has always secretly wanted from the beginning but would never say. It's important for her to prove that she is just as "outgoing" as everyone else. The boys know to "stumble and fall" into her "healing" awaiting arms.

The **poor** girl is planning with her single momma to trap any man of substance for any means of changing their measly existence. Her upbringing and life style is only conducive to trapping someone who will only add to her already menial lifestyle. She gets used often because the boys know that to "show" her a few dollars (not give) will get him his way with her and her momma, too.

Then there is the **wild** girl. She is aggressive, loves sex of any kind, and openly seeks to give herself to any man, boy or anyone who will lay with her. Boys cannot avoid her. They don't have to try to get with her. He is trying to avoid her until he and his boys are drinking and thrill seeking. She awakens from her intoxication on Maury's show, after several appearances, still hearing, "He is NOT the father!"

These girls end up pregnant without any thought of what mothering entails or rearing a child should be like. None of them have any intention of matrimony, neither is anyone of them capable of handling a family. These boys and the girls are young, some uneducated, with no life skills; pregnancy was not a thought. Never read the manual but operating all the equipment. Why does something that feels so good carry such consequences and never-ending responsibility?

Some girls will have an abortion and don't care who knows. I can promise you that everyone who has will struggle inwardly over the murder of that helpless child. While it took only a few minutes to kill and suck that life out of your stomach, that innocent unborn child's screaming has etched its way into your being. That murder you've committed against its poor little bleeding, pleading body; the scars and after effect of it's still screaming loud and clear will never subside or cease from being heard within you.

This emotional trauma is an inward struggle that haunts and taunts as severely as fatherlessness. Believe it or not inward, mental, emotional struggles are very often deeper and more devastating than the outward. Check the mental institutions before you argue this. While the devastating statistics of fatherlessness can be remedied or corrected, the demoralizing act of aborting a child cannot. What you thought was finality will always remain, because a mother killing her own infant never goes away.

I will not mention the two teenaged girls who never returned to school after our summer vacation. Both of them had a wild summer of sexual indulgence that landed them into what they thought was "secretly" having abortions but ended their own lives, a tragic moment for our whole school. What they thought was hidden within the walls of an abortion clinic was so widespread that it affected many of us students, not to mention their families. Aborting an innocent, helpless baby cannot be hidden. The effects of your deadly actions towards its screaming little voice cannot be fixed, masked or drowned out.

The so- called Christians will hide it. The bad girl will tell you, "It ain't your business," while the poor girl continues the family tradition of using the child as a means to land on the "comforts" of governmental assistance with the babies "stuck" living below poverty level. The section 8, Food Stamps, Medicaid and that check which doesn't allow for life, but with all the basic needs covered, it works because it's the over and above. They enjoy a too-long "comfortable rest" under the control of the government. These controls were not established to be family friendly. Many times even a loving father is driven away from the home so that his child can be supported when he is unable, no matter what the reason.

MOTHER'S PROVISION

My mother has given me a pattern for life that I will always be thankful for, even to this day. She had five children and as I mentioned before almost a Baby Daddy to match, but not once did we ever have a meal on our table financed by the government. We have never spent one night in government-funded housing. And everything from a skinned knee to my whole burned up face on Christmas Eve (looking out for Santa) was her financial responsibility. There were times that I wanted her but she was at work making sure that all those needs were provided. She always said that whatever she made of her life was hers to handle; not one child support check, not one government check, although many years she did qualify.

Don't get me wrong. There were times that I had to use food stamps, get a check to cover my basic needs and I had some medical issues and medication for which I am thankful for our government's assistance. These times were utilized to "get back up on my feet" or to cover me while I sought a means to educate myself, a temporary help, not a permanent, generational lifestyle. I have friends who live in the projects whose daughters still live there. The granddaughters can't wait to become eighteen so they can take their children and move into their own government subsidized apartment too.

The government should make rules and laws to govern the length of time to receive these basic needs, only temporarily. For a person during some type of educational program or involved in any

21

form of program to establishing a better life should be assisted, even rewarded. At the time of the initial request for these services the interview should include an expiration date; example:

EXPIRATION PROCEDURES

- Choose an educational facility to attend a college or university or
- Specialized Educational program, nursing, culinary arts, etc
- Open a savings account
- Share Secured Credit Card (cards) to build credit
- Work ten hours a week in that related field (government assist with finding a match)
- We will cover you only two more years (you should be preparing)
- All the money you spend on the Section 8 housing, employment taxes, and your savings account the government will match dollar-for-dollar toward the purchase of a suitable home

Every able bodied person entering any government program should have a date set for an Exit Interview. That date set upon entering (so that it is clear that it is temporary) could be extended after the foundation has been set or for those requiring time for an Undergrad Program or unexpected mishap.

The government is not set up to strengthen the family or relationships, even the Social Programs are not equipped, nor has any program been proven effective in deterring fatherlessness or the effects of it. Parents who have already made the "mistake" of becoming parents prior to meeting their goals, and even those who are self-sufficient MUST realize that their children are red-blooded human beings facing similar (sexual) demands and pressures of today's society. Even more pressure now than during their adolescent years. So parents be realistic about what is actually happening in the daily lives of your children.

All too often I have heard mothers degrade young girls and compare them to their sweet little Christian daughters. These same parents are sitting in the Labor and Delivery room before they would admit that their daughter is actually having a baby. Having all the faith and confidence in your little princess that you "know" this pregnancy stuff won't happen to her is good but you must guard them.

Ask yourself, "At what age did you lose your virginity?" How old were you when you first became a parent? How much confidence did your parents have in you at that time? Did you have access to the "anything you want to know or see" Internet? Was sex so easily obtained, or displayed, or was sexting available to you?

Anyone who expects to be exempt from parenthood or anyone expecting their child to avoid it already knows that this can only be avoided by abstinence (or your unwanted same sex intercourse). If your child is dating, has a Smart phone, or attends an educational facility, you must be realistic. They have access to everything and anything thinkable, what they want and whatever they do not want is pressing in on them all day long. Any chance for abstinence comes through giving careful considering and observing the following:

GUARD YOUR CHILD(REN)

* Watch what comes via the five physical senses

* No touchy feely relationships

* No constant listening to sexual songs and or movies with explicit sexual scenes

* Watch the way your child dresses and carries him/ herself around other teens

* Periodically check the backpack, no such things as my private personal stuff

* Realize that your child is sought after and sex is hunting for them

* Find the scriptures on communications, temptation, protection, etc., and pray daily for them

How to know when it is time to have that talk about abstinence or birth control? You Christians don't kid yourselves because your child is a great target. The enemy is chasing your child down with means of destruction. Schools are teaching alternative lifestyles: homosexuality, sex education is in the text books and on the school videos. With the purpose of destruction the enemy is steadily whispering these things to your child continuously,

"Well, it ain't sex unless it's the opposite sex, you should try same sex because you won't get pregnant, just do it oral so your parents will never know." Your eyes and ears must be open continually watching the signs (but not accusing).

HELPFUL THOUGHTS

* Your child is touching and/or feeling on friends too much
* Your child loves watching sexually explicit scenes
* If you find anything hidden that resembles pornography
* Child constantly listening to sexual explicit songs about sex acts
* Your child plans trips hanging out alone even in same sex circles
* Your child prefers to be alone with one particular person
* Your child doesn't want you to know where he/she is going
* Your child being caught in lies
* If your daughter's friends all have babies
* If there is more than one person of interest, there will be a contest for who will get "it" first, the pressure will be on boys or girls

Ask questions often about their relationships. Ask them how they feel about same sex relationships, too. If they defend it, have open discussions about it. While they should be taught to never discriminate or hate the person, there should be measures to prevent them from even experimenting with it. Preventative measures should be taken to avoid that first sexual experience from being outside of wedlock or just as importantly away from the same sex. The first experience in sexuality is not easily forgotten.

They should be told when you purchase that cell phone that you reserve the right to use and peruse it periodically, at random and do it. Don't try to be the "friend" to your child who does not exercise any authority over their lives.

Birth control is **not a license** to have sex but anyone already driving does need to be properly equipped. Getting married to avoid sex outside of the marriage bed or getting married just to have sex happens all too often. Too many people marry to avoid fornication and commit themselves into an unhealthy relationship and couple up with unbelievers and/ or destroy their futures, sometimes with a person they should not have even befriended, let alone married. Often this hinders a chance of meeting or being available for the right person when they do come along.

MARRIED AT SIXTEEN

One cold February evening in Indianapolis, Indiana, in my mother's living room in front of a pastor who knew neither one of us, I got married as three of my brothers were in the house watching a movie on television. We all knew the pastor was heaven-sent because he was able to squeeze the ceremony in during a commercial break. We got through it, finished the movie, ate a snack, went upstairs to bed and called it a night. We were safe within the marriage bed but had no jobs, no home and nothing that resembled a bank account or any stability between the two of us.

At least I was no longer living in sin and now I called my baby's daddy my husband. What a reason to get married! He was a gentle, very attentive, well-liked only child. He didn't know his father who lived in another state, and seldom saw his mother and like me he, too, was raised with grandmother's assistance. We had many things in common. Neither of us knew our fathers, neither of us knew much of a mother's love, neither of us had anyone to teach us. We had no supervision or parental guidance or direction, we were both uneducated, without money or any job skill, we were both young and inexperienced so we taught each other all that we knew (nothing), and we were both looking for love in all the wrong places, he was the wrong place for me, and to him, so was I.

No matter what I thought at the time, marriage to an unstable, insecure, uneducated boy only compounded my already devastated situation. More, greater, responsibilities, definitely was not the answer. As much as I have heard and believe that marriage is between one man and one woman, I had not heard of any of the criteria or prerequisites for marriage, especially helpful for young couples. A man and a woman inheriting and combining each other's problems is hardly the way to begin a beautiful, productive life, each making life-long commitments in order to enjoy sex is too great a price to pay. In too many cases this eventually causes more problems and creates more responsibilities; mouths to feed, fuss and fight over. Sex alone does not produce in couples what is necessary to remain committed to the relationship for the long haul.

When anyone does not abide by the scriptures that prohibit fornication or adultery, then protection may be necessary because there are definitely consequences that will be suffered.

While I would never condone premarital sex, I must admit that in my situation it would have been much more advantageous to shop for birth control than baby clothes and I only added more problems to my life by getting married.

SCIENCE and GOD

Technology and medical science often work hand in hand with God. In His love and wisdom God has allowed man to create a means of working with medical science to control when married couples become parents. Not every married couple who enjoy ministering love to each other sexually is ready to parent. Getting to know one another, building your lives together, purchasing your ideal home, making provisions for the family, are things that may be realized first. The time to make the necessary provision to be a stay-at-home mother is also a consideration prior to becoming parents. Working together to strengthen your relationship is definitely a means of preventing your child from becoming a part of the fatherless statistic.

Birth control is a defense mechanism to prevent premature or "unwanted" pregnancies without having to kill an already forming child, rather than murdering /aborting a child. God said to Jeremiah, "I knew You before you were formed in your mother's womb." By this we know that he/we are a human being, not just a fetus even before full formation occurs. God said I knew "you" not "it."

You are fearfully and wonderfully made

Ladies: You may be sitting there thinking, I was at the club just having one little harmless drink, just to have some much deserved fun for a night. I was just out minding my own business at the library, grocery store, the park or at home or a friend's house. And a good time you really had until you got the doctor's report. I'm too young for this. I'm too uneducated or too unready. I was planning to travel, get a degree and buy a house and a car. I was just about to make that long-awaited move to my destination. I don't even know the man. I was just out having some fun; pregnancy was not even in my furthest future plans. Wow! Oh, my God! How did all this happen? Now I'm pregnant! What am I going to do?

Men: I just wanted to have some real fun. I was just feeling like I needed to unload. All I wanted from her was a thrilling night. I have too many kids already. It was only a talk game and a few drinks and pills. She wasn't even pretty; not even my type. What was I thinking? Now, she tells me she's pregnant, pregnant? Me, not another kid!

Sperm: We were all hanging out or shall I say, in Dad. We were all just chilling when all of a sudden we were all poured, pressed, pushed out and had to run for cover. I landed in a nice safe place and looked around but didn't see the others at all. At first I was afraid because I was in unfamiliar territory and none of the others were as lucky as me (at least that's what I thought). Every

30

day I was growing bigger and transforming into limbs and organs and forming into something I could absolutely not explain or control. Now I am making thumping sounds like rhythm, having movement and so many multiple changes I cannot understand. When I was with my dad I felt so safe and protected. I was so happy there with father and all the others.

When I first arrived here I was happy and lucky that I finally had my own room and I was fed the finest meals. This space is too confining for me now. Why am I feeling so constricted? Oh, wait, now I am being forced out again. Oh, no I wasn't ready to be slapped on my newly formed bottom, that hurt so bad until I cried out loud in someplace I learned later was a hospital. Hello-o world, it's me, no longer a sperm. At first I was happily living inside of my father. Then he planted me in my mother's garden and I did what we always do when planted...form and grow.

Be fruitful and multiply and fill the earth. The command in those Words sparked life into every sperm inside and seed outside of man. So from the moment this order was issued the sperm sought a womb to be placed into. You can call it love, lust, release, unload, orgasm. You may think daddy was just out for the night and momma was just having some fun, but the truth is: Those hormones are continually working. They cannot be stopped although man in medical science has produced a means of controlling it; birth control.

Don't get me wrong. Let me make myself clear. I am definitely **not** saying that you should go out and have sex anytime with anyone you please just to fulfill your lustful desires, just as long as you use birth control. **I am not!** The only place I will advocate sex is within the marriage between one man and one woman.

I believe God intended that the strongest most powerful physical, sexual experience a male and a female can ever "know" is to be shared together to begin a marriage between a husband and his wife. There is a welding together at this moment like no other time in your life. How many people, male or female, still remember their first love? Still caught up on that person with whom they shared their first orgasms? Trying to relive that magical moment… I so believe that God wanted His man and woman to reserve that special event to weld their love together? And that is what marriage is all about: a welding together that magnetic union where two become one flesh.

A man should leave his father and his mother and be joined to his wife and they shall become one

TROUBLE IN PARADISE

Now that they have become Abraham and Sarah, God's timing for their promise to be fulfilled. Thanks to Sarai (Abram too), unfortunately, they have an issue with another woman and another child still at hand. So now we see the results of two people initiating their own plan, (woman leading) wrong people and incorrect timing.

This union has produced an angry wife, Baby Momma acting out, Father in the middle of an unfortunate situation being torn between two women, and the little innocent child in the middle, without any say in the matter, without any fault of his own, fatherless. Fatherlessness began as early as the Old Testament.

I would venture to say when we learn a lesson from Abram and Sarai, there would be a drastic reduction in children living in homes without their fathers. The figures for substance abuse, premature births, abortions, suicides, incarceration and these other affected areas would be totally different as a result. Not allowing our lustful desires to dictate our course in life, with the wrong people and proper timing are so important that there are lessons and examples for us as early as the biblical history.

People, especially Christians, all over the world are talking about Father Abraham and his wife Sarah and patterning their lives after his riches and his faith. But there are not enough of us talking about Abram and Sarai and remembering the lessons they taught. Sometimes there are great lesson in learning what "not to do" also.

KNOW YOUR ENEMY

Pastor's wives all over the United States are having their women's meeting to learn how to satisfy their husbands, be good homemakers, serve their churches and be good "First Ladies" of their husband's churches. I read all the flyers they post on the Internet all the time. Some of the most educated, influential and prosperous women in our society are in the lineup to share their ideas and teachings. I am still looking for a meeting to attend where a prostitute, a baby momma, divorcee and/or the Other Woman is on the speaker's roster. They sit in judgment of these women, don't like them and avoid them whenever possible. Not taking into account all of the things they could learn from them. One of the wisest things they could do for themselves, their marriage, and not to mention their children is to learn the tactics that their opponents uses to ruin their families.

Often we're wrestling against an enemy and fighting in a battle not seeing everything at face value. We are in a competition daily hoping to win a victory. The sports industry in every category for ball games, wrestling, or boxing, will take the time to preview the actions, strengths and weaknesses of their opponent. To know your enemy's moves is to your advantage. You should not be ignorant of her devices. Knowing where to land a punch or to avoid them could make the difference between whether you win or lose.

Sometimes there are great lessons to learn from those who have failed. If you are willing to listen to those who have been there and done that it could keep you from making some costly mistakes.

Get wisdom and it will keep you

MEN, MAN UP

Husbands /fathers all too often are allowing their wives/ women to dictate how they run the church, their families and all the issues in their lives. What has your Bible said to you? Haven't you read time after time since the Garden of Eden, what happens when a woman leads the man?

Ok, ask Adam (Eve), Samson (Delilah), Judah (Tamar), Isaac (Rebekah), David (Bathsheba) Solomon (wives). The list goes on and on of the women leading men and their outcome. There is a distinct difference between consulting and giving/loving your wife, coming into agreement over things, than allowing her to control or be the head of your house and ministry. Don't get me wrong, you must consult together but you do know what is proper and fair concerning your obligations and your calling. This is not a call for any husband to use unnecessary brutal force or to make or ask her to submit and follow ungodly directions. This is a call for you to examine yourself and seek God for His directions concerning how to lead the church and your family into His divine plan and purposes. It is YOUR duty in the sight of God.

In many cases repentance is sufficient to move forward. But in EVERY case where you have fathered a child (even if you are already married) forgiveness doesn't release you from fatherhood. You still have a certain obligation to fulfill concerning that innocent child. Whether it was born before, during or after the marriage, the

35

obligation is still exactly the same. You bring it, bought it, you own it. For the rest of your life and that child's life, it is your child. I had to stop here and pray because this is a VERY SENSITIVE issue you have made and brought upon yourself and too many innocent victims will suffer. There are some things I did not want to say or add but the Lord knows it must be said to husbands, wives, mothers and fathers step parents who continue in a relationship knowing there is an outside child.

No, that child is not outside of it; correction, that has been the problem far too long. That little innocent "overlooked child" may be the most important person in your life someday before you die. He/she must be brought into your relationship and family just as if he/she were born into it (they were). Like it or not! Mother/wife, IF you choose to remain with your good man who made an awful mistake, you must make allowances for that child in his life, yours too, if you are a loving, forgiving, woman.

Father-husband you must make allowances for that child, make provisions emotionally, physically, spiritually and financially. You may have to give your wife a moment to transition, and pray that she does but one thing is very clear. You will be held accountable for any misuse, unfair dealings with that child and any other (the same thing applies if it were the wife's child, hard as it may seem, men).

The stone the builders would not use has become the most important

But be fore warned, there is a penalty for mistreating any child. *It would be better for a person to have a heavy weight hanging around their neck and be thrown into the sea than to hurt a little innocent child.*

My mother, Marie was not even acknowledged in her father's home. As small as it was he never touched her or even looked at her, and would not allow her infant to be bought inside his home. Because of his lack of concern for her my mother labored for five days with her oldest son until Grandma finally got a doctor who had to use forceps to pull him out. she almost died in the process.

Out of eleven children, eight of them lived to be adults, four boys and four girls. When both of Grandpa Grady's legs were amputated and he was seriously ill, it was my mother's house that he had to live in. She carried him three full meals upstairs each day, made certain he was cared and provided for. She did not receive anything from him, and not one of his other seven children contributed any money for his upkeep.

I was awed by her ability to forgive and serve the man who overlooked her in her early years. Just think of the hardships she must have faced as a teenager with a child of her very own without her father's protection or direction. Although she was the most mistreated, she was the only one to be there for him in his time of need. I have never seen it fail. The child who is the most neglected somehow is always the one that can be counted on the most.

37

The child you love the most and in whom you invest the most of your time and attention may not necessarily be the one to assist you in your time of need. Not only that but you never know what that child will grow up to become. He/she may be the one to "make it big" or become the one in the best position to help you. Pouring love into a child is your best retirement plan. Don't try to play any games or do anything for them out of impure motives because they will know it every time.

TO BE OR NOT-TO-BE

Hear me fathers, that child didn't choose you. It was your irresponsible actions that placed you in that position of fatherhood. In spite of how it happened it was your sperm to be protected and placed wherever you choose. Take the responsibility upon your own self.

There is an interesting story in the Bible that I read years ago as a young lady. At the time I asked, "Oh Lord, why was that even put in the Bible?" To me it was just gross. But the story was about a man whose father charged him with the responsibility of fulfilling his duty of producing an offspring for his brother. But because he knew it would not be his own child, he refused. So, what Onan did was spill his semen on the ground in order to keep from producing a child.

Oh, "So, Ms. Grace, are you saying that I can have all the sex and as many women as I want just make sure I spill my semen on the ground?" **No** absolutely not! What I am saying is this: You are responsible for your own semen. Where they go, or shall I say into whomever they are spilled, is absolutely in your control. You can't expect a woman to do that for you. For whatever reason a woman who is deliberately trying to trap you she is not going to be honest with you (*I'm on the pill or I can't have any children*). If you are influential, make good money, have a great job? Good looking? You are a target.

For someone wanting to destroy your ministry or your home, there is no limit to what they won't try to extract from you to trap you and/ or ruin your reputation. Discrediting your name and reputation is always on the devil's agenda. As many athletes, pastors and ministers who have fallen into that same trap, it still baffles my mind how men never learn from the mistakes they see all too often.

What Onan was saying is this: The child won't be mine to love as a father. I cannot control my time of being with the child. I cannot hold it, love it or raise it in my home. If I cannot be there on location to make the decisions to govern my child's life, protect, provide and care for it, I will not have it. Every man should consider it an insult to him to have another man take over his sperm. Taking his sperm after it has grown into a child is no different, worse if anything, to think of the things that other men (women too) are capable of doing to children. Very often the mother is doing her best to raise that child not knowing that even some of the men she brings into her life, they (boys and girls) are raped, molested, battered or suffer ill treatment by other men. The point is he took control; to become a father or not to become one was his choice.

Far too many wives have looked into the saddened eyes of their apologetic husbands who have committed the ugly act of adultery. Now he is forced to tell his wife through tears and agony that he has fathered a child (without her). The unfortunate act of his pleasure seeking or yielding to temptation has produced something that for the rest of his life and their married lives together, whether long-or short-lived, must take the responsibility for fathering. Protecting and providing for this obligation has forced several demands upon all of their future lives both financially and emotionally.

There are several elements and perspectives to explore in the lives and minds of these family members. No one wants to address this uncomfortable situation but it takes place all too often. So like it or not, know it or not, willing to admit or not, too many secrets are left uncovered in families far too many generations. The television and motion picture trillion-dollar industry exposes, in live and living colors, the things that people do everyday but do not want to admit is happening in their own families. Very often the thought to write these stories and sitcoms derives from someone's experiences.

From which of these perspectives are you viewing this issue? And let's be clear, there is an element of fatherlessness revealed or concealed in each one.

Wife's perspective: Everything that he needs is right here. Whatever he needed sexually I would have provided. We have a home with financial needs, our children to provide love and support for, and he has spent his time with another woman. That's money away from our already struggling household. How much am I willing to allow our children into this mess? Must I suffer as a result of his unfaithfulness? How much of his other life will I tolerate? Will I say I forgive, knowing I will not be allowed to forget? Will I forgive and live in regret? Will I still bring up my frustration every time he leaves this house to go to see that child? What about his relationship to that child's mother? What am I going to do? How can I refrain from retaliating against him for this? Well, after all he's done I feel that I am justified in all actions against him.

Husband's perspective: I have to do something to make my wife realize that she's got to give me another chance. I can't move out because It's cheaper to keep her. How am I going to pay child support? I'm not capable of making it without my wife's income, so I have to ignore the child so I can appease her? Every time I try to do the simplest thing for my kid, I gotta put up with my wife's nagging attitude. What am I going to do about time with this child? I can't make my Baby's Momma unhappy because she may try to take me to court. I will just try keeping everybody satisfied for as long as I can.

Child's perspective: Momma, where's my daddy? Why my daddy ain't at my school or my games? Why does my daddy act like he don't know me sometimes? Who is them other kids he has with him? Why he didn't get me no present? Where is daddy at this Christmas, momma? I been waiting for four hours and just like last week, I know he ain't coming. I know he don't care about me. I hope Momma don't make me go over there. I hate going there it's a waste of my whole day to be around him and be completely ignored.

New Wives perspective: Well I know my husband had children from his first wife but I don't care. I want absolutely nothing to do with that situation. I don't want his children to come here to visit him. In spite of what I told him earlier, I don't want to see them at all. I don't even want him to see them either. Every chance I get I will make certain that I block all communication between them. Well if I have to be bothered with that child in order to keep him I will but I aint sending her a dime to help support her and all them other kids.

Absent Father: I know I got kids here and there but I can't support and visit 'em all. They suspended my driver's license so I cannot get over there (or get a job). I can't bring them to my house because my wife won't allow me to. She won't even let me put any of my kid's pictures on the wall in the house. I know I owe her a thousand dollars but last time I tried to give her fifty she told me where to go, so I ain't giving her nothing. She moved and didn't give me the address so I ain't looking her up. Oh, I know I work with her brother but if she wants me to see my son she'll give me the address herself. Forget it all. My best ain't good enough for them so, forget it. Let her get money from her ole man. I give her money here and there when I can. How do I know where she spending my money? Every time I see her she got a new Louie Vuitton, some new shoes and driving a better car than mine.

Abandoned first child: If I had not seen the pictures on Facebook, I would not have known my father got married. I haven't seen him since then. He is a good father to them kids. I saw photo albums of them all at the games, cookouts and other family outings. On the wedding video he even gave away his stepdaughter, the bride. He bought a car for his stepson, even taught him how to drive. I ran into them at the County Fair together last year; that's the last time I saw him. I know he saw me but he didn't speak just smiled as they all passed by. I never been to his house but I saw it during Christmas all over Facebook with the decorations and gifts for everybody but he didn't give me nothing. He didn't even call me to say Merry Christmas. My father only calls me when he needs my help. I mowed his lawn because his other son wouldn't, but when they go on family vacations or any fun event I am never included. His wife has made certain that all of his inheritance is left to them. He said he told me so I wouldn't be surprised or try to get anything from them.

There are entirely too many Abrams bearing children without having reached Abraham status; men all over the United States have followed this pattern, producing children but not capable of fathering them.

Although Abraham had to send his child away, in his love, He did provide for the care of the child and his mother. They were not sent away empty handed, with no provision.

Mothers, society, government programs and the multi-million dollar Agency called Child Support cannot make men into fathers no matter how many children they produce. The Nationwide Child Support system has done nothing short of create chaos. I would venture to say that that system has just as many problems as it has solutions. From the court system, court personnel and computer information system it has been reported from coast to coast just how short it has fallen. The media continuously reports of their failures and mix-ups.

Whoever came up with the idea to name the agency Child Support and deal with only the financial aspect of it, evidently was not a product of a fatherless home. I do understand, however, that this too is a sensitive subject and that some men have to be forced to do their fair share. It is my guess too that the Child Support Financial System has driven more wedges between fathers and mothers that wreaked havoc on the life of the children-in-the-middle than their own personal issues. Fathers and mothers are arguing over child support before they argue over the divorce. Police reports of people who are missing or killed, children's faces on the milk carton and lives in ruin all over America because of the present monetary system.

Let's review this system in light of United States fatherlessness figures. So year after year the child support system calculates figures to prove that the child is receiving the means to eat and have a roof over his head. I know from receiving it myself that this is the about the extent of it. Meanwhile, the fatherlessness statistics are steadily escalating, increasing in hardships in the lives of those same children.

Fatherlessness is affecting them financially, yes, but emotionally, mentally, and socially as well. Since education is declining so is the likelihood of becoming incarcerated or institutionalized, and so is the risk of committing suicide greater without him.

Although the child support shows the father is providing his continued financial support, the statistics are escalating, and more severe problems are compounding. So even if his money is going there since the situation is unchanged, this proves that the mere lack of his presence is the greatest issue Not only do we see a decline in education but we can also see a pattern of a potential recycling of the same fatherlessness reaching into further generations as fatherless homes continue to recycle. Therefore, the emotional, mental and well being of children is obviously as important to them as money. While we measure limits and set boundaries for monetary amounts to be paid to a child there should also be provisions made for their well being as well.

A CHILD's SUPPORT

A child's support should not be limited to money. While the government is monitoring the affected by fatherlessness it should be responsible for programs and agencies to combat and/ or alleviate this fatherlessness issue too. Something should be researched and set in motion to encouraged men to participate in the lives of these children.

- The end of the Court Order should be automatically programmed into the system so that no one has to use work hours to come into the office, or petition the court to be released from or change the order

- When a father is unemployed and is willing to provide care for the child it should be considered in lieu of jail time (this is cost effective in two separate institutions)

- The system should be linked into the Work Source system so that when an unemployed father is seeking a job, his SSN goes into that system, that history is provided and he should not be jailed when he is actively seeking gainful employment. Sitting in jail is not an avenue to employment

With all the modern technology, Internet programs and new computer software there must be something in place to prevent the chaos. The Court personnel and the system should be working as much to combat fatherlessness as they are at collecting and distributing money.

It's human nature to rebel when being forced; no one likes to live having a noose tied around their neck. Forcing someone to do anything becomes an issue. And enforcement is exactly how it is viewed. Perhaps the father would feel less pressure and be more willing to financially support his child and give of himself more under these circumstances. Children want to feel loved and wanted, not as if they are a great burden to their parents. Everything parents feel is directly or indirectly transferred to the child.

Please don't take this as if I am condoning deadbeat dads. I am not.

Of course there will be some fathers who will not care or be willing to do ANYTHING for their own child. In this case anything or by any means necessary he should be forced to pay towards financing the life he is responsible for bringing into this world. I do admit there will be some working hard to abuse any system. The above-mentioned thoughts are injected for these purposes:

- That the Child Support System will at some point realize that child support is more than just financial.

- That the system will be built upon something more substantial than just dollars

- The system will seek ways to remedy the time and procedures to modify changes

- The child support system be updated to more modern and advanced techniques

- Governmental information systems linking together to provide

47

better and instantaneous adjustments and changes without hardships

- Men who have paid child support to women for "another man's children should be reimbursed in full

- The same system that calculate dollars should also calculate time spent with his child, it should considered in lieu of jail time

Here's a situation where a couple is prematurely placed into parenthood. Yes we both know they asked for it, did what it took to get there. But here is one of their perceptions of the system and its effect.

The Child Support System: The father had all of his children and their mother living with him for ten years but the calculator was still adding and the clock was still ticking but we couldn't fix or make any changes until we could get it on the court docket for the changes. Even then we have no way of calculating the difference. We got word that he was not the father after the child was five years of age but unless someone goes through the proper channels our hands are tied. No we cannot make the mother repay the accused father, that's not a part of our job. We don't have the manpower to answer all the issues we face on a regular basis. He was in the office but we were not authorized to make any changes or reductions but we can see that the child is over nineteen and we did copy all his receipts. The list goes on and on of the changes we need to make but it is not done that easily.

Child Support Paying Father's perspective: Well, she wanted a hundred dollars and since she pressed the issue that's all I'm giving her. I been paying my hundred dollars for the last ten years and that's what they're getting. She made me lose my job and I've been catching a bus too long. There's no way I am going to take a day off from my job and go down there and wait in that line, go to court and modify no papers to give them more of my money. Since they done suspended my Driver's License and made me spend thirty days in jail, I am too mad to give them another dime, besides me and my family got to live too. My last check was for $0.00 so why did they even give me that? I know he's my son but these last ten years has been hell for me. I get mad all over every time I think of what I'm going through on account of her and them folks.

Child Support Receiving Mother: I've been getting that same one hundred dollars for the last ten years but my rent is now double what it was then. How does he think I can make it with this little check he's sending here for his son? He was six years old then and now at sixteen, he eats more per month in groceries than I receive in that check. I need to get more now but I will miss a day of work that I cannot afford. I cannot keep up (my bills) so how can I catch up? When I call them, they keep me on hold for fifteen minutes then I'm told I have to do everything in person. His father needs to come and straighten him out cause he's making me so mad with his disrespectful self.

Child Financially Supported: My father may send me money but momma is always complaining about how broke she is. I never see or get anything out of the check that he sends. Whenever my dad calls he always has a way of reminding me that he is giving me money EVERY WEEK. I asked him for some new sneakers for basketball and he always says get'em out of that check I been sending you all these years. Momma is always fussing at him and he is always mad at the world. He never has anything nice to say and she looks at me like she is always mad at me too.

This system has no way of doing the things necessary to alleviate any of the hostility that it creates in the lives of the families that it serves.

ILLEGITIMATE NUMBER FIVE

Mother had already had four sons by three different men. My drunken father was the only one who stayed around long enough to father three children by her. The brother next to me had a twin sister who died after only three short weeks. Mother said she had not properly developed and was never expected to live. When she died there didn't seem to be any remorse.

She was struggling with four sons, two of which there was no mention of or contact with their fathers. Now still struggling with a man who was more drunk than not, she is now faced with pregnancy number five and still no husband. Oh, no, not again! So when I came along (only the "replacement" that she didn't need). I can imagine how much she regretted being pregnant again. She confirmed my suspicion early in my life by verbally repeatedly reminding me that she wish I had died like my sister. She never referred to the child as her daughter. Although she lived for at least three weeks, I'd never heard her name mentioned.

My dad left her soon after I was born. The "lightness" of my too-soon-developed skin was their demise. He didn't stay around long enough for my skin to darken. Of course it did just as she told him it would. I was thirty-eight years old when I finally found a Marriage Certificate stating that he had married someone else on July 3, 1949, I was born March that same year. During the early stages of our existence there weren't any gestures of love shown to me or either of my brothers, and not one visit from either of our fathers.

My two oldest brothers never knew their fathers at all. The third one did know his dad but was a young adult when he made his acquaintance. Richard and I always knew from whence we came but there was no interaction until we were both young adults too.

ABANDON

(to desert, forsake, or to give up on completely).

Being abandoned by our fathers was devastating blows that none of us ever mentioned. We did not ever speak of the men we didn't know but momma let us know each time we crossed a line what their children meant to her. Although as little children we all grew up knowing about our separate, different fathers. I loved all of my brothers and they each held their own unique space in my heart and life.

My oldest brother, Jerry was the smartest man I've ever known. He could fix ANYTHING. He could build a house from roof to the foundation, everything inside the house and every kind of vehicle on wheels He could fix or drive. Jimmy was the one who was always there with me when I was ill. He taught me how to skate, swim and pushed me to run fast. When I got the chicken pox and measles, I'd scratch and cry and he would cry with me. JC was Mr. Perfect and wanted me, the only girl, to be a frilly, ladylike pink-dress -wearing, proper girl. Richard was next to me. We did everything together; we were inseparable, my protector.

We all shared the same abandonment. It did bind us close together. We were each other's allies because having something in common was comforting to us. We all understood each other, cared for each other because we always knew no one else would. My brothers never fought. Wrestled, yes, but never fought with any ill will toward one another. I found great solace in having big brothers. There was never a time that either of us ever expected our fathers to show up. We had accepted our life as it was, not liking it or wanting it this way but living with it. As often as I wondered how my older brothers felt not even knowing who their fathers were, not once did I ever ask either of them for fear of bringing their pain to the surface.

There is someone who will not abandon or destroy you or forget you

REJECTION

(To refuse to accept; repudiate; to deny)

Each of my mother's previous men had abandoned her with a child , so throwing my dad out and being left with two of his children wasn't the option of her choosing. She had been looking for love every since her father's rejection. Grandpa Grady was there. He didn't abandon Grandma Eddie Lee with their 11 children, (at least while they were still young), thank God.

But living in the house with him for all those months without one word spoken to her had taken its toll on her. Grandma went outside and got her baby and insisted on him being bought back into the house. With this outrage, she had made her plans to leave. Because she was in labor for so long she was too exhausted to even realize where the child was at first. Upon feeling well enough to walk, she left home at the ripe young age of 16, baby in tow.

There couldn't have been a Baby Shower, proud announcement or any happiness to either of my parents when mother became pregnant for the fifth time, with me and still no ring on either finger. Even then, I am told, he was an alcoholic. He and his sister's man ran a Still in the country and brewed their own Moonshine. It was a wonder they made any money because my father and his sister were both heavy drinkers. Daddy was one of the small town Drunks, who was usually stumbling around uncontrollably. He and mother had their fights usually over his habit because she never did drink.

Abandonment has its finality. With time you bury the dreadfulness of it because you're forced to live without. But the horrors of rejection; that continual cycle of someone being present but repeatedly demonstrating their disgust for you, having to face the ill will, ugly words, and negative attitudes. It's like someone constantly having that knife juggling around inside that already awful painful wound over and over again; assaulting that injury. When that hurt that is never allowed to heal, it festers and mounts without relief. This wears down and destroys the soul and any belief system, never allowing you to reach up. Very often I wondered which was worse. I never had to choose because I was privileged, I got to live in both worlds.

Very often the same children that are abandoned by their fathers are forced to live their whole lives in a world of rejection with their mothers. Not necessarily by the mother, with her. I'm definitely not saying that my mother was always rejecting me. But the horrible truth is that even the times that I'd like an ice cream cone or a pair of shoes like other girls, that she couldn't afford and she would have to say, "No", I would feel that same ole ugly rejection. In many forms, many times it was staring at me. It is an harassing feeling that returns continually, without remedy.

Rejection has a evil spirit attached to it that although at times it may not be visible but it is pressing against the mind and holding a dead bolt grip on the child. Sometimes it may play out in a physical ailment and sometimes psychological. Countless mothers are taking their children to doctors who are prescribing medication for something that cannot be diagnosed or cured with medicine. Every busy child is said to be suffering from ADHD (whatever that is) and every slow or melancholy or withdrawn attitude in school should not be diagnosed as a Learning Disability.

Some days a child may be in remorse thinking over the fact that his father didn't show up, another may be hipped up because he finally saw his dad for the first time in a while. During a few doctor's visit it is viewed as an illness rather than an emotion for just being extremely happy.

At other times children are deeply wounded over not ever being able to understand certain things that happen at their house. Why am I always wrong? Why is it that every time I have a fight with my brother it is always my fault, NEVER his? They never allow me to explain my side. Why did I call front seat but I was made to get in the back? When my sister calls it momma remind me that she's sitting up front, instead of me? I just didn't eat my cereal today because I gave it to my brother to let me be first next time? Even after I paid him my food, he still didn't let me go first. Why am I always last? He explodes as soon as he get too much pressure built up in him. Rather than sibling rivalry all these things were viewed by that child as rejection.

Father's gone. I don't even expect to see him any more. It's been since I was six, I'm sixteen. Now without a call or a letter I just gave up on him. Not seeing that desire for father is still buried inside of him and it is as if the mother is secretly to blame. So everything momma doesn't even know to do is mounting up against the only person close enough to lay all the blame. Now that child is growing rebellious, because all of this time the mother is feeling as if she has done her part, just being there.

There is someone who will not reject you nor with hold His love from you.

Fatherlessness has various and profound effects on each child individually. It often drags into the home the dark, ugliness of the past.

The injuries suffered in that relationship that he inflicted upon mother, is still spilling over onto and seeping into the life of that innocent child. The wounds and scars of their past and the devastating blow that finally severed the relationship still hangs inside the house and mother relives each one each time she stares into the face of the "burden" that she is left to bear alone.

The sperm that was the only one to find cover has finally realized in his loneliness that he still alone. The security blanket that covered him has been diminished, and his luck has unfortunately either run out or was the kind that he was better off without.

Wherever there is fatherlessness there is some degree of motherlessness in various forms, too. Don't think for one moment that fatherlessness stands alone. His abandonment breeds in mother a continuous rejection that is so real until it has its own life; living and breathing as much as if it were another sibling. Think about the influence of having Abandonment and Rejection as your big brother or sister. Don't overlook them as members of a fatherless home because it has become very obvious by the stats on fatherlessness that they are the family's most generous, and loyal playmates.

If your father and mother forsake you, there is Someone who will be there for you

More than once I'd be in school fidgeting with my little short hair which I did often when I was trying to remember an answer. Whenever I would find it feeling as plastic as my baby doll's hair, I'd know that it was dried blood. Sometimes rats would bite me in the top of my head while I was asleep and I wouldn't discover it until I was already in school the next morning. As embarrassed as I was for anyone to notice, it didn't seem a big deal to me at all. This had become a common occurrence. But it was still better than me sleeping in the bed between all my brothers.

Daddy didn't see my face but he fumbled into his pockets and gave me all of his money. When I awakened in Indianapolis later that day it was all still in my hand. Even in my misery and sleep I had held onto it so tight until I almost stamped imprints of the president's faces on the palms of both hands. When I counted out his fortune, my self worth was measured out and it ended with the last penny. So for the rest of my life I knew and acted as if I was worth less than a dollar. I later found out what the words low self-esteem meant. During those days it meant worthless.

Even with my father's fortune I was still stuck on worthless. My little proud attitude because he gave me his all sometimes had me hyped up. All the while inwardly there was the knowledge that I was held captive at less than a dollar. The extent of his fortune was the extent of my demands or expectations. His love I measured by the extent of that conversation that we never had. Until I saw him I was capable of living in my delusion, but since that day something had

58

awakened within me. Something that drove me to seek what I didn't receive on that visit. That fiery torch that melted my reserve as we headed to his house left me dripping with anticipation of love. I had to find a way or someone to lavish it upon. So my search for his love, something that didn't exist, began.

Those words that I so desperately want to say to him still need to be spoken. The feel of his hands and a smile was now vital. By the time I was twelve I looked almost sixteen and it took all of my brothers to keep me in check. For a few years it worked. I thought there was a handle on my affections or quest for it. I did well as a student but my cry for attention, or was it affection, got me into trouble far too often. Although I was one of the fastest runners in my school, my attitude was such that I was not trusted to represent our school so competition outside its perimeters was out of the question.

Let me put your mind at ease right now by answering the age-old question of which one needs their father the most, boys or girls? We all know that *it is the one* who didn't need a father to be born. When I need his protection, my brothers crave his love. When I craved his love, they were in need of protection. When I was in need of affirmation, their longing was loving approval. I know I was desperate to run my hands up his sleeve and feel his big protective, muscular arms; while my brother needed those same muscles for a proud embrace. For me the touch of his hand was to sooth, but for the boys it was to train. Everything I needed from him so did my brother, but perhaps for a different reason; no less pressing and no less needful.

There was no way I could speak for my brothers nor access their needs or requirements. All I knew was that for me as a daughter, there was a deep desire within me to receive his love, while my brothers surely could have benefited by learning how to give it, when to give it and because of the absence of his love, surely they'd learn from whom not to withhold it.

At this point my unspoken request has been blown up into an all-out quest for love. Since I had no experience in that field I wasn't capable of defining or realizing what it was or was not. My crippled mind manufactured such a lack of self worth that it debilitated my vision and thinking processes. I wasn't sure if this was better than just not acknowledging my presence or existence or not. That dried blood in my hair was from being bitten by rats during my sleep was no more than I felt I deserved. Thank God I never got sick. Even when we finally moved from that house in the alley into a better place it never elevated my estimation of what I thought of myself. I fought constantly and was very disruptive and disturbed. My cry for attention had overlapped into other areas of my life.

So at the age of 15, right on target, just like my mother, I too became pregnant and delivered my first son when I was 16 years old. To my surprise, after his birth I found that his father had already fathered another child. We had three sons together. Life was a constant struggle for a young uneducated, indigent mother and father. We lived most of our married lives with our families. I continued on with mine, he with his. Obviously we met in the middle at least two more times.

THE END TO MY BEGINNING

As late as the evening had grown I had not been able to find an escape from my present situation. I was visiting a friend who had a mentally ill brother. Seems I had been singled out to render him some sexual favors. As desperate as I was for love this wasn't my idea or place to obtain it. For endless hours I tried to find my way out of this house, trying to press past him, but he was as solid as a brick wall. He had strength that seemed unnatural.

But finally God made a way of escape. The door swung open wide and he walked in. When he realized my unfortunate awful position he opened that split second moment for me to get out. Then he accidentally, on purpose quickly placed himself across the threshold to give me the advantage to escape. Running my fastest but he still caught up with me to be certain of my continued safety as it had grown very dark.

It was Ben, we had been friends for some time but since he seemed to have interest in my friend, Frankie, I had never entertained even the thought of looking in his direction for any reason. So as we walked along I noticed that he was soft, kind and reassuring. He even possessed a protective personality similar to my brothers. What would I have done if at that precise moment he hadn't stepped into my situation? A few days later he passed our house as I was in need of aspirin to alleviate a severe headache. He provided them and I was most appreciative.

Ok, so the other night he assisted me in a great escape. That was a big deal for me. Getting me some aspirin when momma was at work and I was hurting was another one. I was mentally adding up the points and finding myself sinking deeper and deeper into his debt.

What is love except someone to help me, walk me home and make sure I feel okay? I was inwardly building my own demise. Why is it that a person who is starved for love can manufacture it in the smallest thing? He had not placed any demand on me. He had never made even the slightest hint of a request from me in any form for payment. And yet I felt that I owed him my life, myself.

There I was an innocent, 15-year-old feeling desperately stuck and obligated to him with absolutely nothing but myself to give. At 18 years of age, he reaped a handsome reward just by finding himself in a situation where even a peasant would have been a welcome guest. What was to be a one-time payment crash landed me so deep into the motherhood game until, I hit a complete home run with all bases loaded before I realized what happened.

There for the next almost forty years I would wander around aimlessly, only an unseen, unknown guide whispering so lightly in my ear until there were times, looking back, I'm sure I was hearing incorrectly. Although not a victor I was a survivor bombarding the gates never knowing what existed on the other side. Not equipped then and it never dawned on me that not one person ever told me the requirements for becoming who I was already forced to be.

Was there any way to return to being who I started out to be? I searched for the next several decades, first of all, to find out who I wanted to be, but never found myself. How could I answer when I didn't even recognize who or what I was being called? Not knowing where I was headed, so if I should reach my destiny I would never have realized it. Life took me to the places where it wanted me to go. I had surrendered all my options in order to meet one obligation. What I served up didn't come with preparation or reservation. I, without any thought, exchanged my entire being to meet an obligation that wasn't even mine to pay. Now here I sit at the end of an era. This end has taken far too much, far too long. Whoever said we get too soon old, too late smart? Soon never comes and smart is never wise enough. My obligations have full-blown lives. My obligations I'm still struggling with, seeking to oblige. My obligation all my own, no one, not even he, could bare any of the expense. If ever you attempt to pay an obligation not even knowing the price, your life will be poured out into oblivion. When the obligation is never yours, it takes death to repay. It is because of death, his death, that I am finally free. Free for what? Free to do what? Free from what?

Am I living in a limitless environment? Freedom is an expression without limitations. How do I take this freedom and stretch it into a life without boundaries? Today, beginning this day, right now, I will, I must, it's imperative that I press, strain forward with extreme urgency at this appointed time. Take hold of the dreams that were solely mine during the days when only possibilities lay ahead of me. The same possibilities that are now decades old, that never left and had always laid there unhidden. Now I am left to soar, up, up far above all the rules and into a realm where they tell me that only the sky is the limit, those who will force me past the obstacles and stumbling blocks that I'm now overlooking. Perhaps it's because now the reality of that day, finally dawns, that moment and place in life God initiated an eternal plan (one that I would later repeat). Now I see that somewhere, someday in the distant, right now future that I could not see or that I was too blind to recognize then is an ever- present wonderful reality of life to settle into, to make it my own way of life. My obligations are now obliging me and it is they, the obligations for which I once surrendered my all, that will lift me far beyond the sky and without any struggle into a heavenly state where not only freedom, but a limitless life overtakes me... *November 2010*

The life I'd made for myself and how it began when I was a young teenage girl in 1965. I didn't realize just how I was affected until I wrote this in 2010, the year that my son's father finally passed away. Three of his children and almost four decades later I would look back and see how much it cost and how my children landed into a life without a father when I attempted to pay a debt that wasn't mine to repay.

I had just latched onto the only good thing, no matter how small it was, that ever happened for me. Once his "good" treatment exceeded my built-in dollar-self-worth amount, it captured me and I followed it into the unknown without knowing where I'd land, that whirlwind swept me up and captivated me. Coming to my senses to the tune of "three children later," life had carried me to so many disagreeable places that it willed without my being able to control it in any direction.

I remember years later being involved in an incident (not accident) on the highway. We were traveling to church (to serve God mind you) when the Crown Victoria my son was driving hit a water pocket and it hydroplaned on the road. The car spun out of control, made a 360 in one direction. My son, Garrett, in his defensive driving expertise turned the steering wheel in the opposite direction hoping to level out the direction of the car, when it circled around 360 degrees in the other direction. The car skidded off the side of the highway and careened down an embankment.

During that uncertain ride, before the car came to a complete stop, this thought flashed through my mind: Lord where will this ride end? What will be the end result of this trip? The out-of-control and still whirling motion left me anxiously waiting for what we would face for the rest of our lives.

It wasn't directly, solely, their father's fault. He didn't plan to leave his children in a fatherless home. He had absolutely no plan at all and neither did I. In fact, children were not even thought of by either of us. There we were, two fatherless teens together with no thought for where we were headed or any idea that we would be taking children to the unknown places where we could probably be forced to spend the rest of their lives. The life we made, or shall I say the lack of life, for our children wasn't one where neither fault nor blame was to be laid. We had inherited from our fatherless existence no life at all to pass on. The obstacle that lay across our paths we had neither the brains, strength nor wherewithal to hurdle. And absolutely no avenue carved out to find our way around them.

He was the only child of a fatherless home. A family and children to him were welcomed playmates. As many children as he could produce and I could "push out" was all a welcome change that he delighted in without any regard whatsoever to how we would manage their upkeep. To this only child it was an end to his loneliness and the beginning of a role he always wanted to play. He was finally thrilled to hear that magical word "Daddy" around the house.

It didn't matter to him how many buckets we had to use to catch the water from the leaks in the roof. How long he had waited to just hear "Father;" it was like an ointment that soothed his entire existence. As I agonized over how we could keep a leak-less roof over our children's heads, he took pleasure in rehearsing over and over to me his dreams of how big our house would be someday and the golf cart we'd need to ride up to it when our helicopter landed. Life we could only enjoy in a fantasy on the television or in his too-often dreams. He slept too much, often his escapism...

Awakening from his pipe dreams I set out once again into the unknown to resume my search. No matter how big and beautiful our home "would be" it wasn't enough to keep me locked into his dream. Reality had finally set in on me and I still had a void to fill and a hunger to satisfy.

After the birth of my third son, four years later, I wrapped up my swollen milk filled breast, shielded them with plastic bread bags, just for protection, and returned to school ready to get that long awaited diploma. I was so thirsty for that next level of life because those four years were spent, but not lived in a land I was not promised.

Sometime during the third day of class the plastic bags shielding my breast channeled the milk into my lap, down between my legs. I sat there in class wondering why my bladder did not notify me that it needed to be emptied. I didn't need even a diploma to finally figure out that it was my breast, not my bladder, that was too full. The milk that my baby was at home crying for was in a puddle on the school floor. My embarrassment and hungry baby boy sent me home from school; once again motherhood called.

Years later I would try again and finally graduation day arrived. When my baby boy graduated from Head Start, I was there as proud as any mother could be. It was his graduation, rather than my own, that I attended, which was on the same day. I was happy just knowing that I had finally been issued a Diploma.

It was already plain to see, Dr. Grace Swift, Child Psychologist, my name on a gold plaque on the door at the local Children's Hospital. Just enrolling in the area Junior College, I was already visualizing, planning and advancing toward the day when I'd reach that big front lawn. I could almost see it in the distance and could vaguely hear the helicopter motor running.

All things work together for the good

MR RIGHT

In August the same year, walking across the backside of the Plaza in the dark, a bright light shined on me. No, it wasn't a call to heaven but the bright headlights of a tractor trailer. Sitting high on the driver's seat was the man for whom I traded all my dreams, goals and education. After one semester in college, I ended up married again, to Mr. Right this time.

Mr. Right loved me so much until he told me that I needed no education to cook his meals and clean his house. What happened to all my dreams? THE END. What happened to my gold name plaque? THE END. I could no longer see any sign or my front lawn, certainly not the house. I could no longer hear the sound of the helicopter engine. Two sons later...THE END of my dreams and the beginning of another life for another man...still not father.

So I had finally landed in the arms of Mr. Right. We met one night and enjoyed a casual conversation, strolled a few blocks down the avenue, in the truck together all of one full hour, and on our very next occasion to meet we would set up housekeeping together. It was a lovely place. I was surrounded by a life miles away from a leaking roof. We didn't know each other but our expedition together met some all-time highs. Look at me now, a suburban house and all the trimmings. Flying high for a season and then descended into the worst nightmare. I found myself a victim of the same domestic violence that my mother had endured and even before marriage I had known that his mother had lived in also.

That same ugly brutality that I had endured but escaped from just prior to meeting him had invaded my life once again. The inside of my upper lip had finally healed, the scar shielded, the only evidence was found by my tongue running over the inside of it. Both of my front teeth were broken. One chipped on the end corner and the other one broken at the root, inside my gums, only seen by the x-ray taken when I could finally see a dentist. My swollen face, bruised arm and my tooth prints cut in his fist were the evidence that my inner compass had led me in the wrong direction. Instead of the love that I was in search of, I was met with cruel punishment.

So I am still, forty years later asking myself: Why did I marry into this ugliness? What ever made me think that just because he cried when he apologized and said he can't live without me that this was a place to move and settle into? I must admit that at first it was a good life. Mainly because I had learned how to avoid his pressure points, submit like the Godly wife I was. I had grown to hate merely existing in life that was all about him and his needs; without any regard to my ambitions or any of my desires. Without ever a mention of what I had forfeited to "serve" him, he constantly reminded me that everything we had was ALL HIS and it wasn't long until he would prove it.

There is a way that seems right to man but the end of it is death

MR NOT-SO-RIGHT

One Monday morning I descended the stairs of "his" home to find a handsome young couple conversing in my living room. I only spoke in passing as I was headed to the corner store for sugar for my daily morning coffee. On the passenger's seat was a Bible. Upon opening it I found the name of the same female who contacted me the Friday before. I wasn't even surprised at her telling me that she was in love with my husband. Reentering "our" home I found that she was also wearing the same necklace that I had been presented with a few weeks prior. Everything inside of me partially died at the mere thought that he would stoop low enough to bring his woman into "my space."

I tossed her an unworn necklace, stating to her that I supposed she was its owner. After I expressed to him my deepest heartfelt wounded soul and grieving spirit over his actions, I turned to her. My first thought wasn't violence directed towards her because it was his choice that dealt me that devastating blow. Before I could speak she said, "I am not trying to interfere with your relationship, I only want to be apart of it." Shocking!

Can you imagine the boldness of any person to present any wife with such a proposition for such a relationship in her marriage? At that no further words were exchanged between us as he was making every effort to rush them towards the door. The man they used to pull this off, just as shocked as I was over what we had just endured.

After regaining my footing I was forced to return to him as they had taken our son with them when they all left; his assurance that I would not leave. No matter what happened in my life, no matter how deep the pain, I would not allow any distance or time between myself and my little boy.

But from that incident forward it was regarded as his home, not mine. Returning and forgiving him I was able to go through the motions of his life again, but before I could manage to forget those actions, he had a truck accident. One day he handed me his antibiotics, explaining that the doctor sent it to me, further stating that the accident set up an infection in his body and that it was necessary for me to take it also. His medication, not mine, my name wasn't on the bottle, so I knew it was illegal for a doctor to prescribe medication to anyone he had not met, and just as illegal for me to consume it.

Upon the doctor's confirmation of my suspicions, to keep me from calling him, he had to finally admit that it was his medication to cure a venereal disease that he contacted from yet another woman. I was no longer willing to allow myself to dwell in his home living his kind of life. Leaving the nicest suburban neighborhood, greatest schools and all those nice checks he made was wonderful and liberating to me. I was once again faced with estimating my self worth. Motherhood screamed out loud that nothing was enough. As a child I suffered pain, now as an adult, I had grown immune to it. Yes, I was again facing the unknown. No, the void had never been filled. But even without that degree I was smart enough to realize that no matter what I was in search of it could not be found at his house.

Any lonely person void of love and desperately seeking for companionship will stoop to anything and accept literally nothing. I cannot remember any time in my life being so appalled by a female's low estimation of herself. As violated as I felt to have his woman in my face, as humiliated as I was for her, I knew that I was standing face to face with the "evil" that destroys marriages, ruins families, the most serious cause of fatherlessness: Women.

I could say the other woman, but I did say women, in all their various forms; tricks, schemes, and low-down evil tactics, the ones that no man can overcome or outsmart. From the Garden of Eden to the housing projects and penthouses, too, a man's only defense against a woman's scheme is another woman, one who recognizes her game plans.

Before I get into the area where my sisters will either hate me or tell me that I went in too deep, it is imperative that I express one other issue. I would be remiss to overlook these issues concerning our American children's fate while we are trying to be "Politically Correct" or follow the new modern family's way of Life.

AMERICAN CHILDREN'S DEMISE

All too many American families have set the age of eighteen for their children to "get out on their own; to leave their house!" We are so eager to rid ourselves of our sweet little untaught, moneyless, children. They are no longer surrounded by parent and /or siblings but thrust into the open arms of gangs and many other influences. From the provision of a parent into the quickest and easiest provision made available. They are now easy prey; immature, lack life skills, and can't even balance a checkbook, if they had any money in any bank. They are set up to fall into a lifestyle that leads to another generation of fatherlessness. Very often they left home already set up for failure, to return later with a family, if they are lucky enough to escape the jailhouse or the grave.

Has your child been properly prepared to meet the obligations and responsibilities of life apart from you? Can they negotiate a deal or recognize one? Have the two of you had that conversation so your child knows what to do when he/she reached "that" limit? Have you spelled out the boundary lines? Have they been made aware of the wicked plots and schemes of evil? We are not only fighting flesh and blood, and every element they will face will definitely not be at face value. Have they been taught how to decipher the difference between a sweet innocent smile and a wicked smirk?

Can he or she distinguish the dividing line between right and wrong in the text books or the streets? Does your child know a way of escape or when evil is pulling him/her out into gray areas? If your child is an athlete, does he or she have proper discipline and time management skills? If your child is an Honor Student does he or she know that their student circle should be made up of those who are already motivated to study?

Your children are sent to live with roommates because they cannot financially afford to live alone. They have no savings, no checkbook (Debit Card) and their name is not even listed at the Credit Bureau. Some leave home to attend colleges and universities that teach them things you have not taught them any defense against. They are sleeping in a bed next to someone who is yearning for them all night long. They may wake up wondering why they have certain thoughts or dreams; thoughts with origins that they were unaware of. Your child is drinking in impure motives during the night as he/she sleeps.

A battle is in progress over their bodies and souls that they don't even recognize from unfamiliar rooming partners and others: professors, students, and from both sexes. You have no idea how many things are set to devour them every awake and sleeping moment, where you have released them into.

Every person on the school campus is not a student sent to learn. Some special interest groups are sent there with alternative agendas: religions, lifestyles and new age propaganda. Teach your sons and daughters before they leave your home to submit to authority, obey the rules, not to accept easy handouts, and to stay away from what appears evil. None of your children should be roaming around alone. Make certain they are warned to keep in plain view and within the safety of a crowd, especially girls.

POWER'S IN THE COUPLE

The truth is a child is to be kept in the loving, caring, protective confines of home until they are financially capable of providing their own housing and/or trained to handle their own future or given into another protective covering: marriage. Mother's nurturing provides for the physical needs of good holistic health and healing, teaching them life skills inside the home. While the father's training, instruction, and provisions strengthens the soul via peace of mind; knowing that they have the protective covering of both parents is comforting and security. It gives them confidence and builds their self esteem. The perfect balance for life and the future success.

FATHERS WARNING: BEFORE MARRIAGE

The father is watching out over the masculine influences and mother for the feminine ones. Father and mother is the unit for the protection of the daughters and sons; that perfect balance required for proper growth, protection and covering for children.

When those young males approach his daughter he is covering her, protecting her from the game that he already knows and has played himself. In most other cultures that man has to come through the father before he can "have" his daughter. Father usually won't release his daughter into less than he himself has provided for her. She's not allowed to leave a home for an apartment or a three-bedroom dwelling for no less than four. That father is there to make certain that his daughter is provided with more than she leaves home to obtain. No downsizing and no backward moves and fathers usually leave that future husband with the promise that, "If you harm my daughter, there will be consequences and repercussions." This promise alone will definitely decrease the number of fatherless homes.

Too many unprepared young boys are moving into places were women are already "set up" (usually government housing where they share no financial responsibility) and they find that nothing is required of them except to make appearances and render sex, very often his services are provided in more than one place.

This is a perfect example of a person in a reproductive mode but cannot meet the requirements for fatherhood. A disadvantaged, at-risk uneducated male who is still irresponsible is avoiding fatherhood (and should be). Often in his upbringing there is a lack of respect for a "real successful woman" and he finds her more of a threat than a blessing.

"He who finds a wife, finds a good thing and so obtains favor from the Lord." Favor he cannot see or understand because it is a supernatural endowment and cannot be seen or recognized by a man seeking pleasure or "handouts." When he is given supernatural favor on finances, open doors, extra money, and even witness miracles, he will discount it by reasoning it out in his own thinking. He would not want to put any effort into making a good life in a good home but will often settle for the projects and or an easier way out. All too often a male is looking to live on Easy Street not realizing that it, too, has a dead end.

EASY STREET

Before I was divorced in 1987, my husband had been living with another woman for more than a year. They were active participants in their church together. I saw her daughter's wedding pictures, where he walked her down the aisle. She called me often to tell me what she would do to me for causing him problems (I remind you he was MY husband). But I continued a relationship with him. Plainly speaking I continued to have sex with him. My stupid reasoning was that we were still married so I was supposed to. He would very often come over to the place where I lived or sometimes we'd actually spend nights at hotels and even take trips together.

Finally one day I asked him, "What are we doing, if we still love each other and want to be together why don't we just do that?" Our "hanging out" and sexual encounters ended when he said, "When I am home with you, I've got all the responsibility but with her I'm on easy street." I'm not obligated for nothing. I can come and go as I please, my plate is in the microwave, whenever I show up, and I don't have to pay for nothing unless I want to." We had children between us but they did not. Of course he had obligations; our sons were his responsibility. I released him to Easy Street and while we were yet married sometimes he'd take the boys to Easy Street with him on weekends.

While I never wanted my sons to learn any lessons on "Easy Street," I would never deny them any time or opportunity to be with their father. It was important to me that I upheld him in their presence and whatever fights or disagreements we had I shielded from them. They still have no idea of some of the things I've suffered as a result of his violent behavior toward me. Unless they were present during an altercation I would hide it from them. Later on in our marriage they saw the violence, sticks, guns and damage to our rented house and personal property that he and his woman's children brought to our home.

It became so bad that when their father came to the house our little five-year-old boy would wet his pants. I am glad they weren't there to see that last battle when we both landed in emergency. After several blows to my body with the instrument he used to check the air pressure in his tractor trailer truck tires, my sons landed a blow between his eyes that left a scar that he will wear to his grave. Blood was every where but because he was my baby boy's father, I would not allow my older sons to end his life, although they had the means by which to accomplish it. With this our marriage and our relationship was completely severed. The long awaited, dreaded end had descended upon us.

Remembering my stepfather's words at the end, made me wonder what his wisdom and protection would have done on the front end of that lovely night that those bright lights shined upon me when I met Mr. Not-So-Right-After All. His words, the only advice I've ever heard from my step father, came when I had left my husband to his own life style. He caught me coming out of the bathroom, looked straight into my eyes and said, "Get yourself together and then make your move." Those words carried such weight that I never forgot the spot where he spoke them from, still a very relevant, priceless piece of advice for daughters and sons.

MOTHER'S ADVICE

Just as fathers maintain a watchful eye over his girls, so mothers are there to provide the expertise and direction to their sons where other women are concerned. It's so sad that men don't listen to mothers when it comes to other women. Sons too often disregard mother's advice, thinking that her expectations are just set too high. They're not taking into consideration that she can see in another woman what a man will never see, or in seeing he won't accept. How many headaches, how much heartache, problems and even unprepared-for children could have been left unborn if they had only heeded the advice of their mothers? How many sons are fathering children that are not their own biologically, that they find later in life and sometimes not at all? But unfortunately the woman who sleeps with a man and then intimately lays with him usually gains the advantage.

All through the wisdom of Proverbs sons are warned to avoid a loose woman. A loose woman is one who has no limits or boundaries. She stops at nothing to have her way, submitting not just her body but her smooth conversation which is full of honey (manipulation, deception and lies, anything attracting). Every wife patterns and prides herself on the model example of the "Proverbs 31,"wife and that's great. But before all her accomplishments were her directives to her son. "Son," she said, "Do not spend your strength on a loose woman."

Men don't be left weakened, rendered powerless (without any defense) with a woman, and do not drink and lose your head or ability to reason. A weakened man, an intoxicated man is like a derailed train, out of control and carries everything trailing him (he's responsible for) into destruction along with him.

Too often a wife in her "comfortable" robe, is smiling to herself, really proud because the husband is knocked out, snoring. After she has ministered to his body, she too is fast asleep now, feeling her duty performed. Unlike the loose woman who utilizes all her "talents," ministers to his whole body and then she seeks to gain his soul. In her costly attire, gold jewels, painted lips, secrets, scents and aromas she's now stroking his ego and sitting at his feet, giving him a feeling of superiority.

Every asleep and waking moment she lavished her full attention upon all his desires. How often he is awakened by her in a "position" where he is totally defenseless and rendered powerless to control his "appetite." The look of seduction is in her eyes and her ever stroking moves she drives him down any avenue at her command. He's even ushered into fatherhood with unbridled passion without any thought or reservation. He's enraptured (trapped) caught up in the heat of her moments.

At first just to win him over, she is always eager to cater to him and experiment with every sexual ploy and fulfilling every fantasy he can imagine. While he is asleep she is still hovering over him, rubbing and caressing, too. Her greed and desire is mingled with aggression that's overwhelming him. Now to maintain her control over him, she continues her devices and stops at nothing, not even childbearing. For a loose woman there are no limits if there are any restrictions they will be set by her.

How many misplaced sperms are planted into the womb of a loose woman, misled by a weakened man? Look at how much destruction his intoxication has produced, and her selfish desires created. Matrimonial cords and relationships are severed by hearts being intentionally broken, thereby creating even more Fatherlessness because having and rearing children he never considered or mixed into this equation. Although within her there were absolutely no limitations; whatever it takes. Like Tamar, who disguised herself as a prostitute and tricked her father-in-law into getting her pregnant and then she set him up.

Man has given away his strength and now he finds himself in a relationship, so weakened that he will forever be at a disadvantage, and perhaps grow weaker still, never able to regain his strength or control over her or their situation. The power she held over him from the beginning will continue throughout their relationship as he has relinquished his position of authority. The longer the relationship continues, the stronger and more power and control she gains until he and all that he has is totally disregarded. There's rarely much love in these relationships. He's locked in for her convenience or to fulfill her "whims" because a woman seldom finds real love for a man for whom she's lost all respect.

You cannot understand why you so easily mistreat your wife. She's pulling you away from your children, leaving them in pain, they don't matter. She uses up all your time, displays a different attitude when you want to do something for yourself. You see those overwhelming statistics and you still take no initiative to be there. You know your child is hurting and you're saying, "Well, they didn't call me, I didn't know it, it was out of my control, it's not my fault."

Everything is what she says; you cannot imagine why everything is for her and never anything is for you or those you've fathered. You cannot even make the decisions for yourself. Why you're struggling with every little thing. She is so busy with everything else until you always have to wait. She's made plans that included your help but you never even got the memo.

BEWITCHED!

Oh, foolish man, she has bewitched you! Like those foolish Galatians; church people who should know better, are now caught up in the flesh. You are living in confusion, suffering medical issues for which there are only short-term remedies. You experience accidents, mishaps, and are never able to gain any footing. That manipulation and deceitful loose woman that you have allowed to control your life has surrounded you and clouded your vision. That rebellion, manipulation, and deception has become as the sin of witchcraft over you and you actually wonder why your plans always fail.

Bewitched people never realize it. Even coming face to face with its harsh reality will not, sometimes cannot, accept because it's hidden behind a smile and occasional good deed. Now and then she throws you a bone, sometimes even in public to keep you under her "thumb/spell/control." Yes, you are driving from the back seat.
Side note# some of you men of the cloth have controlling women too. There are too many of them **controlling** lives, men and the churches, too.

- That one who is in/over every ministry in the church

- That one who wants/ does everything her way

- The one who makes the church's plan instead of the pastor

- Does everything at church and nothing at home

- She undermines/ changes things after you have made a decision

- Made decisions that you are not aware of until they're initiated

- Display a different attitude when things don't go her way

- One face for church and different one for home

- Always has to be seen and her voice heard

- Finds fault with anyone who doesn't follow her lead

- Very often instigate means for others to retaliate for her

So we're back to that night of pleasure and that sperm that made its way into the womb and is now a child. A child, or children born into a situation that he/she was forced into without any act or choosing of his or her own, Born into the lives of two people who are strangers, ill suited, not ready yet, or out of time. Unfortunately not one person alive was given the choice of who the parents are. But how many children are made to suffer, overlooked, rejected or even hated by their own parents?

Unfortunately too many children are born in this environment. Even they do not have a voice and are pawns in the game of this life or lack thereof. They too must maintain their place of submission. They have no voice, they receive very little attention and very few, if any, answers as to their existence. Their loving care is only in direct proportion to their obedience to the directives. Those by products of the flesh must always yield themselves to the control of that evil spirited person.

Feeling it only appropriate to attend the funeral of the young man that I had married at the age of sixteen, I went. Since our sons were pall bearers I left them to sat near the back of the funeral parlor. I assumed my sons would remain up front but they did not. Following them to my side were a few other young men, who were pall bearers also. Conversing with one of the young men, I learned that he had been my stepson. He was born four months prior to my divorce from his father.

When I asked him his name I was surprised to find that although he was 33 years old his last name was not the same as his biological father's, my ex-husband, but another man's. I was then astonished to find that his parents had never told him the reason. He was never given an answer to any of his questions concerning his own birth. He had his turn to be rendered speechless when he learned that, although his mother was a preacher when she gave birth to him, she was not even married to his father; I was. His biological father and I were still married when he and at least two of his siblings were born to him. How often has our story been repeated (even in the churches)?

It is the operation of a supernatural controlling spirit that cannot be detected in the physical realm by the natural eye. Every element conjured up by that evil spirit must be discerned and/or controlled by a person who is, In HIM, Christ Jesus. Natural man has no defense against the devil who has been with God, ministered to God and has been alive for that many years. He is reaching himself through these individuals; sometime they themselves are not even aware they are being used. Because they have been deceived, that spirit of deception continues to operate through them. It was the female who was deceived in the Garden of Eden and deception is a "craft" she received long ago.

Being in Christ Jesus, who was with God from the beginning, is the one and only place of safety and surety against that control or that can successfully handle it. When a woman who is deceived comes face to face with a woman who recognizes that evil spirit, she is frustrated, disturbed because of the presence of God that she cannot tolerate. This is the place where you must remain steadfast in Christ displaying HIS attributes, so that she realizes you are not at all intimidated by her (evil spirit).

Too many wives have had to face her and stand their ground. Confronting her is sometimes necessary, very often it happens more than once; she's not always easily silenced. It's not always the same female; but it's that same spirit but resurfaces in different faces. She is bold, make no mistake about it. She is so sanctioned by the deceiver until she has the audacity to believe that she is right or has some rights. She may even be willing to publicly oppose you. While a Christian wife may not want the embarrassment, she thrives on it. I told you that the spirit in that female called me and told me what she would do to me about messing with her man, he was still MY husband. Go figure!

Too many beautiful women are wondering why their husbands are involving themselves with the likes of that ugly woman. She has absolutely nothing to offer and most often the wife is much prettier, and hands down more wonderful. That's because for many it is not always the outward appearance that captures him.

Don't get me wrong. There are men who are hung up on pretty, sexy, young things. Everything in his pants is motivated by looks. The fake hair, fake lashes and fake nails, shapely good-smelling body and a nice smile moves him. Satan has his number too. He's often juggling a wife, a girl friend and all those in between;

sometimes sisters and other female relatives too. It's possible that some malformed bodies are such because their parents are blood relatives. He has children who are siblings that are also cousins and some who don't even know each other. Many times those that do are at odds with each other. (Frankly speaking, if it were not for the parent issue they may find a beautiful friendship).

He will have any woman who is weak, starving for affection or stupid enough to share him, usually at her expense. His money, time, sex and family are all so stretched out until there's not enough to go around and no one is satisfied. The devil will use anyone and any tactic to wreak havoc in family relationships. Whatever it is you're looking for, Satan will cast a character that will fit perfectly into your play in a supernatural form to bring people under his control.

From the time of birth, if a child is allowed to be born, until hospice, families are robbed of the sweet little moments in life that families used to cherish. I remember having my little boys in my bed with me during the night. Whenever they would cry I would pull them closer. If it was a hungry cry, trust me I'd always know, because the sound of his voice would alert my system to supply his food. His mere cry in my ears would cause the milk to form in my breast. I would breastfeed him until we were both sound asleep together. I'd still have him neatly protected under my arm and full of mother milk. Now mothers are no longer allowed to sleep with the baby in her bed, the milk comes from a cow or is formulated from a laboratory.

When we'd go on trips I'd hold them in my protective arms and sing them songs all along the road. They weren't strapped into a car seat where they were already getting used to restraints. We didn't use play pen to confine them but they were allowed to enjoy the house as we trained them the places to enjoy at their will and the things that they could not handle or that did not belong to them. They always understood the difference. I disciplined our children with words and/or facial expressions so there was very seldom a need for punishment. However if I needed him, "Big Brown" was always a threat that one way or another they diligently sought to avoid.

Once my husband was rushed to the hospital and we were in the waiting room for an excessive amount of time, but my three little boys sat in their chairs and never moved without permission. While I was in with the doctor they knew not to leave the chair until I returned. When I did a nurse said, "These little boys sat here like Tin Soldiers, I have never seen children so disciplined. What did you do to them?" Because they were disciplined at home, it showed outside the home as well.

So now the same government who is calculating fatherlessness statistics is the one who governs how we sleep, ride and discipline our little ones. In today's society parents send out their children from infancy throughout their adolescent years to Day Care, Child Development Centers or other educational facilities, onto Public Schools (very often), Middle School then High Schools never knowing how much they are influenced by all these different personalities. The curriculum is one thing (you need to beware of) but the life and character of the people teaching them is important too. We fail to realize over the course of their lives how many different people are shaping their lives.

Considering the school hours, sleeping hours and your work schedule, compare how many hours you spend with them and how much of yourself is injected into your child. Do you touch, caress or embrace them? When do you minister your love to them in even small ways? Are you looking into their eyes when they talk to you? How many opportunities are you given to pour your unconditional love into them? You should always be the closest and greatest influence on your own child. When everyone else has an angle, prerequisite or a reason to care about them, you should make it known in no uncertain terms that your love is unconditional.

Never allow your ill feelings for the other parent to affect your feelings for your child

- Never retaliate to the point where the child is affected
- Never tell your child how "No good" their parent is, even if it's true
- Presents never replace your presence
- Treat each other with the utmost respect in the presence of the child
- Plan a consistent time for you and the child each week (daily if possible)
- Don't withhold discipline over something you are guilty of doing; use it as a learning tool
- Teach your child what you want them to be even if you fall short
- Give constant encouragement to your child
- Find a slogan that is just between the two of you; use it often
- Remind the girls how beautiful and great they are
- Teach them that anything they didn't work or pay for they don't deserve
- Remind the boys how strong and awesome they are
- Find out early in life what your child wants to become and shape him/her early into it

- Look for mentors to shape them into professionalism early
- If the father is absent, develop a friendship with a positive male role model for him
- Teach them to submit, NOT rebel, against authority
- If they tell you something is wrong, CHECK INTO IT

It is of utmost importance that you began shaping your child's life and future at an early age. The most powerful and the greatest athletes are those who began practicing at an early age. Most of the successful performers have little videos of the early days when they stood singing in front of an audience. Those adults didn't begin at the teen stage of their lives to shape their futures, but rather during the childhood days, very often the earlier the better.

One of the main concerns in our country is Law Enforcement and/ or the Criminal Justice System. It is with deep regret that it is so widespread and so much time, money, effort and people are so deeply concerned for the "correct" treatment of criminals rather that the avoidance of crime. Every agency and person in America, from the president, FBI, DOJ, attorneys, judges and churches too are in the media arguing and talking about the ill treatment of criminals. The same people who are hurting and wounding innocent people in our society are crying about how they are being abused.

Our country is divided, spending countless dollars and using unheard of amounts of energy because those who are selling drugs, that are ruining families, causing destruction in too many areas of life, those who murder, sexually molest children, rob and steal from innocent families are not willing to accept the same. While we're not overlooking it, it would be a new day and a wonderful place to live if we all gave equal time into demolishing fatherlessness.

How many of us are fighting or protesting to attend a university or for advancement in education? How many different agencies,

LONELINESS
(depressing feeling of being alone, secluded)

Loneliness will accept almost any companion: gang, family, sometimes even sexual gratification. After hurting, seeking and searching for so long, any thing or person who can offer even a momentary substitution can be misconstrued as loving. In all too many cases people are seeking a source of gratification although it may not necessarily be physical, but will settle for any type that temporarily alleviates that inward struggle. The only problem is that because it's so temporary it must be repeated continuously. A continual visit, hit or drink.

I had never thought of loneliness as a child being so surrounded by a family with all its many issues, loudness and involvements. Upon listening and understanding my cousin's loneliness I had to come face to face with my own. In doing so I was reminded of movies and how a character would be surrounded by a vast crowd and everything would go completely quiet. Although the person is engulfed in so much activity and movement he was not hearing a word, everything was irrelevant. Loneliness causes one to see him or herself as irrelevant. Your whole life is totally of no consequence. No matter how vigorously you wave your hands, shout or reach out, there's no one to even care.

Because of my close relationship with my cousin, Billy, I was also given a panoramic view of loneliness and its effect on a young child's life. I wasn't familiar with the life and inward struggles of an only child. The only one I grew up knowing was Billy. He was actually closer to me growing up than my brothers because we were the same age. He longed to be at our house in spite of our struggles. He'd rather endure the constant look of dissatisfaction displayed on mother's countenance, and even more so towards him, than to be alone.

Billy had all the "finer things" in life. All that we lacked, he left at his lonely fatherless, and sibling-less house. He was always striving just to "fit in" anywhere and was willing to forfeit everything just to be mistreated every place and every family home that he tried to force his way into but failed.

Our fatherless homes sent us on two different journeys. I didn't realize he had found a source of comfort or a means of escape in substances, and he didn't know I was pregnant. When I was forced to face the realities of motherhood early, and it became all too obvious, Billy was the only person I didn't want to face. Feeling that I had abandoned him knowing his struggle was too hard for me to accept.

While I was hiding myself from him he was hiding his substances from me. So there we were, now teenagers locked into unfortunate situations and neither one of us saw what was coming. Mine was a cover while his was a mask. He would later write a stage play titled: *Oh the Mask We Wear*. In it he unveil the many faces of an Addict; exposing the effects of drug addiction.

I will never leave you alone even if you go to the end of the world organizations or churches are seeking to keep these people from criminal activity prior to being arrested in the first place? The best avenue to preventing or combating this issue is to begin at an early age to shape inner peace and contentment within a young child's heart and mind. Fatherlessness is the main reason for criminal activity. Since we already know the cause we already know where to begin to deter it.

DADDY'S LIL GIRL

There was one man that, although my recollection of him is limited, I will not forget. Mother didn't marry my dad, William Charles (WC) Brown, but she did marry a Brown, when I was very small. Recalling where we lived is my reference point. Next door to my Great grandmother, Geneva Henderson, whom we all called Ma Mitt. Although she was born in 1883, around 1952 she owned a double house and we lived on the other side of her.

The beautiful moments I remember are those moments when he walked through the doors of our house, I could hear him calling, "Where's My Lil Girl?" At this time only heaven knows how that sounded in my ears. Being called anybody's Lil Girl was a shining moment for me. Although I was enjoying the most beautiful time of my life, no one else was. Odorsey Brown was an Ex Military man from Camp Atterbury, not far from Indianapolis, Indiana.

He was a serious gambler, who loved shooting craps. The thing that sticks out most in my mind was the constant fights he and my mother used to have. Once she broke a bottle over his head and cut her hand, too. The excessive bleeding landed her in Emergency. The same Christmas that I poured water down our coal-burning stove so Santa Claus would not get burned was the same Christmas season that he and mother had the biggest fight.

It was so bad that my big brother, Jerry came to her defense. Jerry hit him over the head with a big, hard candy cane so hard that it startled him. He stopped fighting her, which was his intent, to chase Jerry. My brother ran up the steps, locked the bedroom door behind him and jumped out of the upstairs window, escaping into the cold without the proper clothing.

Mr. Brown had taken mother's money and gambled it away, again. Upon hearing this she attacked him and it was all-out war at our house, the one that marked the end. Her second chance to be Mrs. Brown was hereby terminated. Thus sealing the end of my short lived days of being somebody's Little Girl. Pouring water in our stove sent flames up my arm and into my face. My whole face was consumed by flames that sent me to Emergency all night. I missed Santa; if he did show up at all I never knew. But I could not distinguish which was the most regretful, my burned up face or my bruised up heart. If I ever had a low estimation of myself, having a burned up face didn't help. My face would some day heal, but I would never again be called anyone's little girl, and that pain drugged loneliness into my life that would never heal or be forgotten. Like that fire that could not be extinguished.

Some of the relationships that mothers bring into the lives of their children sometimes cause more pain than it is worth to her or them. I sometimes wonder if this is a thought on the front end of a mother's journey to find love. Is she looking for love for herself or companionship for the children? Or, are all of the lives included considered?

The night that I met my Mr. Right, I told him that I had three sons to live for and I was trying to educate myself to provide adequately for them. His injection into this admission was that he was man enough to handle that. He wanted me and he would take the kids too. He had a big truck, a motorcycle, and was man enough. Man enough for me and had the things that boys loved too seemed worth a try to me. He used his Moving Van to move me into my new apartment the second time we met and I handed him a key to the door.

Sure enough, we had only been together for less than a month when he told my sons to call him daddy. I wasn't in love at that point and doubt that he was either. When he came to town I was always home with the boys and we did everything together. We loaded and unloaded the truck. Everything he did, no matter what it was, we were all by his side. After we all began to attend church together, grew to love each other and, in order to do the right thing, we got married.

THE CYCLE RECYCLES

In my wildest dreams I never imagined that my relationship to him would end just as my mothers, in a horrible act of violence and, like hers, that would include the children. My heart breaks to think of my sons suffering the consequences that they suffered. I knew the horrors of losing father after father.

How many mothers are nursing old wounds and continuing to assist and giving in to grown children because we are still trying to make up for the past? How many times do we continue to submit to unreasonable requests because of our own guilt? How many children are still feeling as though their mothers owe them something? How long do you still linger in regret over that scar that tore you away from your father? Is mother still being held accountable?

I worked in a youth detention center for a short season. During my short time working on the boy's unit I met an unreasonable, unusually disruptive young man whom I could not understand. Finally after not being able to keep him out of trouble I got serious with him about his future incarceration.

This child confided in me that his behavior was such because he wanted to be held in custody and sent to the Men's Prison to see his father again. Although he longed to see his dad, who had beaten his mother beyond recognition, he was openly hostile towards her. He refused her visits but was ruining his entire life and future just to see his father who was imprisoned for beating her. How much is a mother required to tolerate in order for children not to have to live in fatherlessness?

Life continued on for mother, we were still at Ma Mitt's house but she was all fed up with us kids, the fights and all the drama that we bought into her life. We confined ourselves to our side as mother once again faced that same ugliness that she lived in at her father's house. Being near someone but feeling rejected more than loved.

HELL-O MR. NICE GUY

Finally on her job she met Mr. Nice Guy. He was a very soft-spoken guy that she could rely upon. Knowing that she had five children at home and aware of how many times her heart had been broken, he would daily bring her treats to work. Because they got together we finally moved from Grandma's house, he retrieved his two children who had been left in another state, so all seven of us lived together, until the two of them had one more son. At some point she became Mrs. Charles Cager. Not any of us knew when, but I always thought it strange that she ends up with someone with my father's name.

It was nice having a mother and a father in the house again after so long a time without it. At some point in their relationship we'd call him daddy. It is important to children to hear those titles thrown around the house from time to time. Somehow they seem to add a nice touch. My stepfather had a daughter there but after my eight or nine years of being the only girl it was hard to share my position. Although I was never his little girl it was okay to me just to enjoy that father figure in the house.

Oh, I can still remember the day that we all got the hit. The wind was knocked out of our sails when mother for some unknown reason, in that tone of voice that we all grew to dislike so much,

Announced, "Charles aint none a y'all's daddy. Stop calling him that!" To this day we never knew what was said or what brought that on but we did receive that message, loud and clear. The End.

So not only was I not ever called anybody's little girl again, I would live for the rest of my life and not have any one to call father, daddy, dad, pops nor anything that related me to a masculine figure. Charles would continue to be a male figure living under the same roof as me and my brothers and yet the fatherly touch was never felt. I don't remember ever touching him or feeling him touch me. For that matter I don't even remember any gestures of love from him directed toward any of us, or mother.

One night we were in my mother's backyard having a serious debate because my oldest son had decided he wanted to return to Indianapolis to live with his father. After exhausting myself trying to make him realize that his stepmother would not allow him there, I succumbed. My specific directives were that since they approved it, he was to remain there. Living with my mother was absolutely out of the question. So our laborious conversation was over my son's education. I wanted his report card but he and my mother were arguing over who had it last. When the truth finally surfaced it revealed that my son had never been enrolled in school. He had spent the entire semester at the age of 15, watching Soap Operas and drinking coffee everyday and living with his grandmother. I was livid.

Right in the middle of my tears my stepfather asked me this question, "Have I ever said anything out of the way to you?" When I was too overwhelmed with my present situation and then got hit with this, too, I was speechless. So he, raising his hand, asked again, in a demanding tone, after I answered, "No!" I was taken aback over that whole incident. Where did that come from and why?
His life was routine and like clock work since he had always worked

It was the Christmas Holiday weekend again. We were passing through Indianapolis on our way back to Rochester, NY, from our usual Florida Christmas vacation, as I sat in the car in a trance. All the family in the car and no one knew what I was experiencing. Christmas proved to be brutal; I felt burned, scared and bruised, once again, but this time sheer devastation had invaded my heart and my mind severing me from yet another father figure.

There was absolutely no explanation for this. I never asked him or mother why he asked that question because it drew its own conclusion. In my mind I wondered if his lack of affection was because of her fear of having a man around me, or if she had made some accusation that sparked his question? Either way I'll never know. All I do know is that as long as I lived near him, whether she was at home or away, he was nothing short of pure perfect in his actions toward me.

But as I traveled back into the days and times of our home I could never find a time that I received any kindness or shared a beautiful moment with him. He never bought me a special gift or embraced me at any time for any reason. Then I was faced with the realization that he purposely avoided any contact with me, and why. At long last it all made sense after being with him since I was about nine years old. His life was routine and like clock work since he had always worked two full time jobs it went unnoticed. Even though he was a great provider he definitely was not at all "fatherly."

Upon hearing that his life was nearing its end, I went to his bedside to communicate my appreciation to him. With deep regret I shared a house with a perfect stranger who upon his dying bed, he was allowed to do something that resembled a father when he administered a father's blessing as me, my youngest brother, Gregory Cager, his youngest son, we all bowed our heads in prayer together.

Perhaps I was lucky, blessed, or fortunate that I was surrounded by gentlemen. It wasn't my choice but it was perfectly suited for me but how many girls (boys too) have been approached or molested by a stepfather or their mother's male friends? How many women have reason to believe that there is an unnatural relationship between their man and her children? Any woman who is unsure of this should not even be involved with any man that she cannot trust with her children. Too many mothers are leaving their daughters with "just any male." Don't be too quick to have men around your daughters but when you do make certain they always dress and act appropriately.

Take the time to teach them what is inappropriate and ask to be informed of anything they are uncomfortable with. Even then sometimes it's hard to know; therefore, make random checks periodically without being announced. Be aware of and watch their attitudes and conversations but don't accuse anyone of anything unfounded. Having a good man in your life is so healthy and great for your children. Don't deprive them of a father's touch when he is proven to be a good man.

There was not one thing left unsaid from that trip in Tennessee from Grandma Susan's funeral to my biological father's house that I had ever spoken to him, as long as I lived with him. There were so many things I needed to hear myself say, and so much I needed from a father that I missed. I was still on that journey while a male was present every day walking in and out of my life.

How many homes have men present who walk in and out of a child's life and never share it with them? All too often men share houses with their sons and daughters but the distance is a gulf so wide until they never express their love, concern or give anything that resembles direction. Sometimes I wonder which is worse, to have one present who is not there at all or one who never existed.

I couldn't find enough tears to shed that could relieve me of the pain that had accumulated over so many years, all the years of my life. Those words were still left unspoken. There were no coins in my hands; this time I was holding the steering wheel, now steering my own course in life.

The pictures I saw of my father walking down that aisle, giving away the bride was one that moved me to tears. Not able to distinguish if my tears were of sadness or joy was my inner struggle. Did he ever learn to father anyone or was it just not me? Either way I resolved to continue forward.

NEVER BEGINNING LOVE

The last argument and every argument from my brother was mingled with real tears, not from wounds he'd suffered from the war in Viet Nam but from the love and the relationship he was never afforded with the man living moments away who, fathered him, yet he never knew. The men who we loved most were those from whom we received the most pain.

At father's funeral all three of us lined up like toy soldiers and happily accepted all the compliments on what a great man our father was. Astonishing that they all knew the one laying there, his life had ended and yet neither one of us knew him. Although he had left his entire estate for us to share equally, none of it mattered. When the estate was settled I suffered one final blow as I was listed on a Legal Court document as his "Illegitimate" daughter. Proving, I had lived out my whole life striving for something that didn't exist.

REAL MEN

There are real men who are strong enough to uphold their word, their family and their responsibilities. They are in control of their own lives and are capable of extending it to cover for the good of others.

But there is One whom my eyes never beheld but His love was all consuming. Because of Him my self worth was no longer measured by coins or any tangible thing. From the moment I realized that I was accepted by Him, my life began to change. My new measuring device was a built-in system no longer holding me captive by what or whom I lacked or how anyone else did or didn't love or care for me. I was no longer roaming about as that sperm who was cast out into an unknown, unfamiliar place and was still seeking the rest of the crowd or trying so hard to "fit in" thereby falling into a gang or another violent or disruptive crowd.

Never again was I allowed to feel or see myself as a "cast off." I no longer limited myself to the mere mindset of being a "replacement" for the daughter who died or the illegitimate daughter of an abandoned father. A transformation had descendent upon me, One I could not hold back, alter, or even repress. It was greater than my thoughts and ran deeper than any ill will directed towards me. I was wrapped up into the One whose love and care for me presses into my being more clarity than the imprints from my father's coins.

The love I required was no longer limited to a man. One day He stretched out His arms as He spoke so clearly to my heart, "Greater love has no man than this…

So just as I cried out so desperately for the love of my father,

He gently spoke back to me…

My darling, my daughter how often I've longed to draw you to Myself
To reveal Me as your Father so you'd need nobody else.
The first time that I saw you, in your mother's womb,
I made sure your perfection needed no more room.
I was married to your mother when you were very small,
everything for life and godliness I gave you both My all.
I've never left you, gave My closeness like a shield,
So every path you went down darkness had to yield.
For each chance you had to know a Father, I was always there,
to love you, to guide you and show how much I care. Drawing you into
my presence, there you could stay
exceeding and abundance of life to enjoy in every way.
Yes, I gave you food, I gave you clothes and everything you needed,
Through every storm, test, and trial I made sure that you succeeded.
Always, I am speaking to you, loving you, showing you what you missed
My everlasting arms, through every storm, you could make a list.
Of the battles won, the things I've done and the times I bought you thru
My lovingkindness, tender mercies and My Son who died for you.
When your father or your mother forsake you, you can trust in Me,
Seeking My face, you will know Father and all He's supposed to be, .
Perhaps you missed a father and all he didn't do
Your eyes haven't seen, nor ears heard what I planned for the children
too. A loving God, a giving father, faith as your Title Deed.
Now, my darling, my daughter, what more could you possibly need?

FATHER'S LOVE…eternally.

My biological Father, **William Charles Brown, United States Army WWII Veteran**, Your war tour; Normandy, Northern France, Central Europe. Thank you for your service, and the War Medallions, but most of all, thank you for life

My Stepfather: **Charles Edward Cager**, our provider. Thank you, sir

Odorsey Brown, thank you for calling me, your little girl.

My brother, **Richard Swift**, thank you for your moral and financial support.

My mother, **Marie Geneva Swift Cager**, mother who fathered too. I thank God for you and the day that you became a new creature and introduced me into a new life of love. I love you mother, thank you.

CPSIA information can be obtained
at www.ICGtesting.com
Printed in the USA
FSHW02n0321130818
51290FS

9 781514 347157